incredible edible Bible fun

Making God's Word Memorable With Easy Recipes Children Can Do

by Nanette Goings

Group

Loveland, Colorado

Incredible Edible Bible Fun
Copyright © 1997 Nanette Goings

credits
Associate Senior Editor: Susan Lingo
Managing Editor: Paul Woods
Chief Creative Officer: Joani Schultz
Copy Editor: Debbie Gowensmith
Art Director: Lisa Chandler
Cover Art Director: Helen H. Lannis
Computer Graphic Artist: Bill Fisher
Cover Designer: Ray Tollison
Cover Photographer: Craig DeMartino
Illustrator: Leslie Dunlap
Production Manager: Ann Marie Gordon

Unless otherwise noted, Scriptures quoted from The Youth Bible, New Century Version, copyright © 1991 by Word Publishing, Dallas, Texas 75039. Used by permission.

Library of Congress Cataloging-in-Publication Data
Goings, Nanette.
          Incredible edible Bible fun: making God's Word memorable with easy recipes children can do/by Nanette Goings.
                    p. cm.
          Summary: Contains recipes, projects, and devotions based on Bible stories involving food.
          ISBN 0-7644-2001-1
          1. Cookery—Juvenile literature.   2. Food in the Bible—Juvenile litera-ture.   3. Bible games and puzzles—Juvenile literature.   4.Christian education of children. [1. Cookery. 2. Food in the Bible. 3. Bible games and puzzles. 4. Prayer books and devotions.]
I. Title.
TX652.5.G545 1997   96-48253
641.5'123—dc21   CIP
                                                                                    AC

10 9 8 7 6 5 4 3 2   06   05   04   03   02   01   00   99   98   97
Printed in the United States of America.

Table of Contents

Introduction

An Adventure in Bible Learning

Stories involving food abound in the Bible! We read of the forbidden fruit in the Garden of Eden, the manna in the desert, the grain and meat sacrifices in Old Testament worship, the water turned to wine at a wedding, the bread and fish that fed the five thousand, and the broken bread of the Last Supper. In many cases, food helped people remember something in particular, and that's the idea behind this book. What a fun and memorable way for children to learn about God—through their sense of taste!

Incredible Edible Bible Fun contains recipes, projects, and devotions that can be used in any Sunday school, Christian school, vacation Bible school, after-school program, or club program. The recipes can be created in the classroom since you don't need ovens, microwaves, or stoves of any kind to complete the classroom portion of the recipes. The activities also don't require dangerous utensils such as sharp knives and electric mixers. All of the incredible edibles are made with easy-to-find, inexpensive ingredients and equipment and can be done in twenty minutes or less.

In each *Incredible Edible Bible Fun* devotion, children will learn not only through their sense of taste, but through all their senses. Your kids will have a great time making these yummy projects and will learn from the Bible at the same time! And most of these activities are simple enough for kids to share with their friends with minimal adult help!

Each devotional activity contains a photocopiable recipe card that includes an appropriate Bible verse. Teachers can send the card home with kids to reinforce what they learned in class. Or kids can create their own cookbooks, adding recipes each time they do a devotion. Simply punch a hole in the upper left-hand corner of each recipe card, and tie a ribbon through a stack of cards. Let kids craft their own covers using poster board and markers.

At the end of each devotion, you'll also find "Extra Fun" activities that directly relate to the theme of the devotion. For example, for the devotion about the vineyard workers from Matthew 20:1-16, an Extra Fun activity is to paint with grape stems and juice left over from the recipe.

With *Incredible Edible Bible Fun,* you're ready to lead kids on fun learning adventures. Just thumb through the pages or scan the table of contents to find the right Bible verses, and then grab a few ingredients to stir up a devotion kids will never forget!

Handy Tips for Teachers

As you prepare for the activities in this book, keep the following guidelines in mind:

Cleanliness and Conservation

- Always make sure kids wash their hands before handling food items.
- Use a clean, damp cloth to thoroughly wipe all surfaces you'll be using. Keep a damp cloth handy throughout the activity, too!
- Involve all kids in the cleanup, and make sure you leave your area in good shape for the next group.
- Don't allow kids to waste food. If there's extra after your project is finished, be sure it gets used, or find someone to give it to.

Supplies

You may want to keep on hand these frequently used items:

- resealable plastic bags (quart-sized freezer bags work best)
- paper plates
- plastic knives and spoons
- measuring cups and spoons
- paper cups
- drinking straws
- washcloths

The Recipes

Mixed-Up Mass
God made the world.

Mixed-Up Mass
Serves 1

Theme to Remember: Creation
Verses to Devour: Genesis 1:1-2

Simple Supplies:

a clean, empty 4-ounce baby-food jar with a lid

3 tablespoons of whipping cream

a plastic knife

crackers

What to Do:

Let the whipping cream come to room temperature in the baby-food jar. Screw the lid on tightly; then shake the jar until a lump of butter forms (about 10 minutes). Pour off the thin liquid, and then spread the "Mixed-Up Mass" on crackers. Eat and enjoy!

(From Group Publishing, Inc.'s *Incredible Edible Bible Fun;* copyright © 1997 Nanette Goings.)

The Message:

Set out the baby-food jars, measuring spoons, whipping cream, plastic knives, and crackers. Ask:

● When have you made something from a blank piece of paper or a glob of clay?

● How did you decide what to make?

Say: **Did you know that God is our maker? The Bible tells us that God created the entire world from nothing. In the beginning, the earth was empty and had no shape. It was a mixed-up mass. God took that mass and formed and shaped it into the whole world. He made oceans, mountains, and sparkling rivers. He made plants, animals, and people. He created everything! God is the only one who can make a world from a mixed-up mass, but we can have fun making a delicious** *treat* **from a mixed-up mass.**

Follow the directions on the recipe card. Be prepared to have kids shake their jars for about ten minutes until the butter separates from the cream. If your class is very large, use a quart jar and a pint of whipping cream, and let kids take turns shaking the jar.

While the kids are shaking their jars, read aloud Genesis 1:1-2. Then ask:

● Do you think it was hard for God to create the world? Explain.

● Why do you think God made the world? plants? animals? people?

● How can we thank God for his wonderful creation?

Say: God created the world from nothing. He turned a mixed-up mass into a beautiful world that plants and animals and people could live in. Let's thank God for his creation with a special prayer. Pray: Dear God, what an amazing creation your world is! Thank you for making the world and for making me, too! Amen.

Let children spread butter on the crackers and gobble them up. As they eat, encourage them to tell about their favorite things in God's creation.

Extra fun:

👋 Let the kids create their own pretend worlds from modeling dough. After the projects dry, have kids use tempera paints to make their worlds colorful.

👋 Get classroom wiggles out by letting kids pretend to be "mixed-up masses." Have children sit on the floor with their knees bent and their arms wrapped around their legs. When you say, "Mix it up!" have kids roll around the floor by tipping on their sides and by rocking and rolling back and forth. When you say, "Freeze!" have kids stay in one place.

Garden of Eden Fruit Salad

God loves us even when we do wrong.

Garden of Eden Fruit Salad
Serves 8

Theme to Remember:
God's forgiving love
Verse to Devour: Genesis 3:6

Simple Supplies:

a 16-ounce can of pineapple chunks

a banana

a can opener

a mixing bowl

small paper cups

a 4-ounce can of mandarin oranges

a 4-ounce box of instant lemon-pudding mix

a plastic knife

a large spoon

plastic spoons

What to Do:

Pour the oranges and pineapple chunks with their juice into the mixing bowl. Use the plastic knife to slice the banana into the bowl. Sprinkle the dry lemon-pudding mix over the fruit; then stir the mixture until there are no lumps. Serve "Garden of Eden Fruit Salad" in paper cups. Yum! Yum!

(From Group Publishing, Inc.'s *Incredible Edible Bible Fun*; copyright © 1997 Nanette Goings.)

The Message:

Set out the cans of pineapple and mandarin oranges, the banana, the instant lemon-pudding mix, a can opener, a mixing bowl, the plastic knives, a large spoon, the paper cups, and the plastic spoons for eating the salad. Ask the children to think about a time when they disobeyed someone. Then ask:

● **What happened when you disobeyed?**

● **How did it feel to know that you had done something wrong?**

Say: **In the first book of the Bible, we're told the story of the first man and woman. They were also the very first people to disobey God. Do you know their names?** Pause for children to answer; then continue. **God created Adam and Eve, and he loved them very much. Like a loving parent, God gave Adam and Eve rules to follow.** Ask:

● **Why are rules important?**

Say: **God told Adam and Eve not to eat the fruit from one tree in the beautiful garden where they lived. But Eve decided to eat some of the fruit anyway. Then she gave some to Adam, and he ate it too. How do you think they felt then?** Pause for responses. **Adam and Eve knew they had disobeyed God, and they were ashamed. God wasn't happy that Adam and Eve disobeyed him, and he sent them away** from the beautiful garden. But he still loved them. God may not always like what we do, but he always loves us.

Let's make our own "Garden of Eden Fruit Salad" to remind us that God loves us even when we do wrong things.

Set up an assembly line, and follow the directions on the recipe card. Have some children be Can Openers, some be Fruit Pourers, others be Pudding Mixers, and the rest be Salad Servers. When kids have finished preparing the salad, read aloud Genesis 3:6. Ask:

● Is it easy or hard to love someone who's done wrong? Explain.

● Why do you think God forgave Adam and Eve? Why do you think God forgives us?

● Who can you love and forgive this week?

Say: Adam and Eve disobeyed God, but God still loved them. When we do wrong things, it's important to remember that God still loves us. Let's close in prayer. Pray: Dear God, thank you for loving us even when do wrong. Amen. Let kids enjoy the fruit salad, and then have everyone pitch in to clean up.

Extra Fun:

🖐 Have each child create a beautiful Garden of Eden "fruit tree." Drop a spot of brown tempera paint on the lower portion of a sheet of white paper. Have each child use half of a drinking straw to blow the paint into the shape of a tree trunk and its branches. Let children add dribbles and drops of colored paint or food coloring to their tree trunks as the fruit.

🖐 Go on a short service hike to clean up the church grounds or a nearby neighborhood or park. Point out that God made Adam and Eve to care for the beautiful garden and that we can care for God's creation too.

Ark 'n' Animals

We can trust God to care for us.

Ark 'n' Animals
Serves 2

Theme to Remember: Trusting God
Verses to Devour: Genesis 6:12–22

Simple Supplies:

a slice of pita bread

jelly

animal crackers

peanut butter

a plastic knife

paper towels

What to Do:

Use the plastic knife to cut the pita bread into 2 ark-shaped halves. Open the "pita arks," and carefully spread peanut butter and jelly inside. Poke in a few pairs of animal crackers. When the ark is full, gobble it gone!

The Message:

Set out the pita bread, plastic knives, peanut butter, jelly, animal crackers, and paper towels. Be sure you have one piece of pita bread for every two children. Ask:

● Have you ever worked with a partner?

● Did you trust the partner to help you? Why or why not?

Say: The Bible tells about a good man named Noah who was given a *big* job to do with a perfect partner—God! God told Noah to build an enormous boat called an ark. Do you remember why God told Noah to build the ark? Pause for responses. God was going to wash the world clean with a big flood, but he was going to keep Noah, his family, and all the animals safe in the ark. God trusted Noah to build the ark, and Noah trusted God to care for everyone inside. And God took care of everything.

Let's make our own "Ark 'n' Animals." Then we'll discover how we can trust God to take care of our lives. Find a partner you can trust to work with.

Hand each set of partners a piece of pita bread, two paper towels, and a plastic knife. Have partners cut the pita bread in half and then take turns spreading peanut butter and jelly inside. Let each set of partners add a handful of animal crackers to their arks.

When everyone has made their "Ark 'n' Animals," read aloud Genesis 6:12-22. Ask:

● **Do you think Noah trusted God? Why or why not?**

● **Why is it important to trust God?**

● **How can you trust God more this week?**

Say: Noah trusted God when he built the ark. Noah trusted God when he filled the ark with animals. Noah trusted God to take care of his family and all of the animals when it rained for forty days. We can trust God to take care of everything in our lives too. Invite kids to gobble up their arks and animals.

Extra Fun:

✍ Young Children will enjoy this finger rhyme.

One was Noah, wise and fair. (Hold up one finger.)

Two came the animals, pair by pair. (Hold up two fingers)

Three were Noah's sons—his crew. (Hold up three fingers)

Four were the wives that came in too. (Hold up four fingers)

Five were the fingers folded in prayer (hold up five fingers),

As Noah trusted God to be right there. (Clap and cheer.)

✍ Play a fun game of Animal Charades. Have each child take a turn pulling an animal cracker out of a box and then imitating the sounds that animal makes. When the other children recognize what animal is being imitated, have them act out the animal's typical movements.

Altar Appetizer
We can thank God for his blessings.

Altar Appetizer
Serves 1

Theme to Remember: Thanking God
Verses to Devour: Genesis 12:1-8

Simple Supplies:

a few large round or square crackers

grated cheddar cheese

a paper plate

pizza sauce

a spoon

What to Do:

Place a cracker "altar" on the paper plate. Spread a spoonful of pizza sauce on the cracker. Sprinkle grated cheddar cheese on the sauce-covered cracker. Your "Altar Appetizer" is ready to eat—but you may want to make more than one!

The Message:

Set out the crackers, pizza sauce, grated cheddar cheese, spoons, and paper plates. Ask:

● When have you expressed your thanks to someone?

● Why is it important to thank someone who helps you?

Say: It's important to express our thanks for special gifts or for someone's help. And it's especially important to thank God for all he does. The Bible tells us about a man who loved God and was faithful and had a heart filled with thanks. His name was Abraham. Because Abraham loved, trusted, and obeyed God, God showered Abraham with countless blessings. And when Abraham received good things, he built an altar to thank God. Altars were places to worship and thank God, and Abraham built many, many altars to thank God. Ask:

● Why is it important to express thanks to God?

● What are some things you'd like to thank God for?

Say: We can make edible altars to remind us to thank God for his blessings.

Follow the directions on the recipe card. When everyone has made several "Altar Appetizers," read aloud Genesis 12:1-8. Then ask:

● How can you thank God this week?

Say: Abraham thanked God often. In fact, he lived a thankful lifestyle. We want to thank God too. Let's say a prayer and thank God for his many blessings. Pray: Dear God, thank you for the great gifts you give us and for the help you always offer. You are great, God, and we thank you and praise you. Amen.

Extra Fun:

👋 Older kids may enjoy using a Bible dictionary to learn more about how altars were built. When they've finished their research, let them make altars from clay or modeling dough.

fuzzy Arms

God wants us to be honest and fair.

---

fuzzy Arms
Serves 1

Theme to Remember: Honesty
Verses to Devour: Genesis 27:21-23

Simple Supplies:

a kiwi fruit

half a banana

plastic knife

a grape

2 raisins

paper plate

What to Do:

Rinse the fruit, and peel the banana half. Using the plastic knife, quarter the kiwi lengthwise leaving the skin on the kiwi so you have 4 "canoe-shaped" pieces. Place the banana half on the paper plate as Esau's body, and place the kiwi sections as Esau's fuzzy arms and legs. Use the grape for Esau's head and the 2 raisins for his feet. Admire your fruit sculpture, and then eat it.

(From Group Publishing, Inc.'s *Incredible Edible Bible Fun*; copyright © 1997 Nanette Goings.)

The Message:

Set out kiwis, grapes, banana halves, raisins, plastic knives, and paper plates. Ask:

● When was someone dishonest with you?
● How did you feel?
● Why do you think being honest is good?

Say: God knows that being honest is very important. In fact, Proverbs 12:22 tells us that God doesn't like dishonesty but respects people who tell the truth. A Bible story about honesty and dishonesty tells us what happens when someone isn't honest. I'll tell you the story, and you can help by imitating my actions.

Long, long ago in the Bible, you know *(hold hands open like a book),*
Lived a man with two sons—Jacob and Esau were the ones. *(Hold right hand up and pretend to touch the heads of two sons.)*
Jacob was handsome, smooth, and clean. *(Rub hand on chin as if feeling for whiskers.)*
Esau looked hairy, tanned, and lean. *(Show your muscles.)*
Jacob's mother loved Jacob the best,
But their father loved Esau more than the rest.
Jacob and his mother planned and lied *(shake your finger)*

To steal Esau's blessing 'fore his father died.
They covered Jacob's arms with fuzzy goat's hair
 (rub your arms)
And asked his blind father to give him Esau's
 share.
Their father felt the fuzzy arms. *(Rub your arms.)*
"My firstborn son," he said. *(Hold up one finger.)*
And then he gave Esau's blessing to Jacob
 instead.

Ask:
● How do you think Esau felt when he found out that
his brother stole his blessing?
● How can dishonesty hurt someone? hurt God?
● Why do you think God wants us to be honest?
Say: **That story was fun to tell and had an important message
about honesty. Let's make our own "Fuzzy Arms" fruit sculpture to
remind us about the story of Jacob and his brother, Esau.**

Follow the directions on the recipe card. As the kids are enjoying
their "Fuzzy Arms" sculptures, read aloud Genesis 27:21-23. Then close
with the following prayer: **Dear God, we know that you value honesty.
Please help us work hard to be fair and honest. Amen.**

Extra fun:

✋ Play a game of Are You Esau? when kids need a fun change of pace. Instruct
children to form a circle. Choose someone to be "It" and to stand in the center
of the circle with his or her eyes closed. Instruct everyone else to hold one of
their hands in toward the center of the circle. To create an "Esau," tape a
piece of felt or fuzzy fabric to the back of one child's hand. Let the child
playing It go around the circle and touch children's hands until he or she feels
the felt. Then have It try to guess who Esau really is.

✋ Play a quiet game of I Was Honest When... Sit in a circle with the children,
and hand one child a paper heart. Have that child first finish the sentence, "I
was honest when..." and then pass the heart to someone else. That person
must repeat what the first person said and then finish the sentence with his
or her own ending. Play until everyone has had a turn.

Dreamy Corn

We can listen for God's guidance.

Dreamy Corn
Serves 5

Theme to Remember: God's Will
Verse to Devour: Genesis 41:16

Simple Supplies:

a 16-ounce can of corn

dried parsley

a large spoon

a can opener

bottled Italian salad dressing

a mixing bowl

paper cups

plastic spoons

What to Do:

Open the corn, and drain off the liquid. Pour the corn into the mixing bowl, and add 2 large spoonfuls of Italian salad dressing and 1 spoonful of dried parsley. Mix the ingredients well. Serve your spicy corn in paper cups with plastic spoons. Joseph's "Dreamy Corn" tastes mighty fine!

(From Group Publishing, Inc.'s *Incredible Edible Bible Fun*; copyright © 1997 Nanette Goings.)

The Message:

Set out the cans of corn, a bottle of Italian salad dressing, dried parsley, a mixing bowl, a can opener, large spoons, paper cups, and plastic spoons. Gather the kids together, and whisper very quietly: **I have an important story to tell you.** Whisper even more quietly. **It's about listening carefully. Can you all hear what I'm saying?** Pause for responses. Then, in your normal voice, ask:

- **Is it always easy to listen? Why or why not?**
- **What sometimes makes it hard to hear someone?**
- **Have you ever heard God talk to you? Explain.**

Say: We talk to God often. In fact, every time we pray, we talk to God. But did you know that God talks to us, too? He often speaks to us through the Bible, but he has spoken to people in other ways, too. The Bible tells us about a time a king had bad dreams but didn't know what they meant. One of his dreams was about seven healthy stalks of grain and seven dying stalks of grain. What a crazy dream! None of the wise men in the king's kingdom could understand the meaning of the king's dream. **What do you think the dream meant?** Pause for responses.

Say: Joseph was a man who followed God, but he was in the

king's jail when the king had the dream. Joseph was wise, and so the king called Joseph to tell what the dream meant. Joseph told the king that although he couldn't understand the meaning of dreams, God would tell him.

God told Joseph that the dream meant there would be seven good years of grain harvest followed by seven years of hunger due to bad harvests. Wow! What an important dream. And Joseph understood the dream only because he listened carefully to God. Joseph became an important man in that country because he listened to God.

Let's make Joseph's "Dreamy Corn" to eat and enjoy. Then we'll learn more about listening to God.

Follow the directions on the recipe card. Be sure to let everyone in class have a part in preparing the treat. When the "Dreamy Corn" is done, set it aside for a few moments as you read aloud Genesis 41:16. Then ask:

● **How can we listen to God?**
● **What can we do to be better listeners?**

Close with the following prayer: **Dear God, you talked to Joseph, and he listened. Please help us be like Joseph and listen for what you want to tell us. Amen.**

Eat and enjoy the "Dreamy Corn"; then clean up the cooking area.

ᖰ Extra Fun:

🖐 Play the age-old, favorite game Telephone. Have kids line up and whisper a message from person to person from one end of the line to the other. Pass messages such as "We listen to God," "God talks to us," "God will help us when we listen," and "Thank you, God, for talking to us."

🖐 Help young children learn the following rhyming prayer to repeat before eating the "Dreamy Corn."

> Dear God, when I talk,
> I know that you listen.
> Help me carefully hear
> So there's nothing I'm missin'. Amen.

Frogs, frogs, and More frogs

God can do anything.

The Message:

Set out the canned pear halves, maraschino cherries, dates, paper plates, can opener, and plastic knives. Ask:

● Who is the most powerful person you can think of?

● Do you think that person can do just about anything? Explain.

Say: The Bible tells us about a time that God showed his power to an entire country. The Israelites wanted to leave the land of Egypt because they were slaves to Pharaoh, a powerful king. Moses asked Pharaoh to let God's people go, but something strange happened. God made Pharaoh stubborn so that he wouldn't listen to Moses. Why do you think God did that? Pause for responses.

Say: Because of Pharaoh's refusal, God was able to show his miraculous power. As one miracle, God sent jillions of jumping frogs into the entire land of Egypt! Oh, just think of it! Frogs in the palace, frogs in the houses, frogs in the ovens, and frogs in the beds of all the Egyptian people. Ugh! According to God's plan, Moses prayed to God, and the frogs stopped coming and went away. In the end, Egypt and Pharaoh suffered terribly—God's power was too much for them. Pharaoh finally let Moses and the Israelites go free. God can do anything!

Let's make our own froggy treats to remind us that God's power is greater than anyone or anything.

Follow the directions on the recipe card. You may wish to set up the cooking area as an assembly line. Let some kids be Pear Placers and put pear halves on paper plates. Have others be Eyeball Attachers and cut the cherries in half and place them on the pears. Other kids could be Leg Layers and place the dates at the sides of the pears. After the "frogs" are made, read aloud Exodus 8:1-6. Then ask:

● **How did God's power help Moses and the Israelites?**

● **In what ways does God's power help you?**

Say: God demonstrated his power to Pharaoh. He caused many miracles to happen so that the Israelites could go free. And God is powerful today, too. In fact, we know that God can do anything!

Extra Fun:

🖐 Play a lively game of Leapfrog to get the wiggles out.

🖐 Learn a fun jump-rope rhyme to do together.

> Frogs in the water,
>
> Frogs in the stew,
>
> God loves me,
>
> And God loves YOU! (Child jumping rope points to another child to
>
>   enter in and jump alongside.)

Instead of "classic" jump-rope, try swinging the rope back and forth just off the ground. This method of skipping rope is easier for most kids and safer too.

Shivery Hailstones
Only God sends miracles.

Shivery Hailstones
Serves 1

Theme to Remember: God's miracles
Verses to Devour: Exodus 9:22-26

Simple Supplies:

vanilla ice cream

an ice-cream scoop

a plastic spoon

flaked coconut

a small paper bowl

a napkin

What to Do:

Measure several spoonfuls of flaked coconut into a small bowl. Scoop up 1 scoop of ice cream, and drop it into the bowl. Use the spoon to roll the ice cream in the coconut until it's well-coated. Now enjoy munching your very own "hailstone!"

(From Group Publishing, Inc.'s *Incredible Edible Bible Fun*; copyright © 1997 Nanette Goings.)

The Message:

Set out flaked coconut, small paper bowls, plastic spoons, napkins, and an ice-cream scoop. Keep the ice cream in a freezer or a small cooler until you're ready to prepare the "Shivery Hailstones."

Say: **Let's play a little game. I'll tell you something that I may or may not be able to do. If you think I can do it, give me a thumbs up. If you think it's impossible, give me a thumbs down. Ready?** Read the following sentences, pausing as children give thumbs up or thumbs down signals.

- **I can fly without wings.**
- **I can eat a bag of potato chips.**
- **I can paint a chair.**
- **I can pick up a mountain and move it.**

Say: **That was fun, but we all know it's impossible to do everything. If I wanted to make it rain and hail, I couldn't do it. But there's someone who can—and did! When the Israelites wanted to leave Egypt and Pharaoh, a mean king, God performed many miracles to help them. Once he sent a terrible hailstorm that killed the crops and injured people and animals. Just imagine the icy chunks raining from the sky! The people must have been very frightened!**

God showed Pharaoh and all of Egypt his mighty power through miracles. And finally, God's power convinced Pharaoh to set the Israelites free.

Let's make delicious, edible "hailstones." Then we'll learn more about God's miracles.

Follow the directions on the recipe card, and be sure to let everyone help make the hailstones. Let everyone munch their treats as you read aloud Exodus 9:22-26. Then ask:

● **Why did God use miracles to show his power?**

● **Who's the only one who can perform miracles?**

● **When do you see God's power working in your life?**

Close with the following prayer: **Dear God, you are truly a powerful God. We thank you for your miracles, and we know that you are the only one who can send a miracle our way. Amen.**

Extra Fun:

🖐 Play a fun game of Hailstones in the Air. Blow up three or four balloons. Have kids kneel on the floor and bop the balloons back and forth while trying to keep the balloons from touching the ground. If a balloon falls, have kids name or look up one of the plagues God sent to Egypt.

🖐 Create your own inedible hailstones. With your hands, mix together one cup of laundry soap flakes and one tablespoon of water. Knead and squeeze the soap into a solid ball. (You may need to add a bit more water.) Place the soap balls on a piece of foil to dry, and then use the "hailstone" soap balls to wash your hands.

Red Sea Salad

God helps us.

The Message:

Set out the applesauce, instant strawberry gelatin mix, measuring cups and spoons, plastic spoons, paper cups, and can opener.

Say: **Let's play a game called Helping Situations. I'll read a situation; then you decide how you could help solve that situation. Here's the first one: Your neighbor is eighty years old. She has a hard time getting around and really needs the weeds pulled in her garden. How can you help?** Pause for responses.

Say: **Here's the second situation: Your mom came home from work late. Everyone is hungry. She needs to make supper, but your little brother just skinned his knee and is crying. How can you help?** Pause for responses.

Then say: **When we need help, it's important to know that God is with us. Did you know that God divided an entire sea to help his people? That's right! Moses and the other Israelite people had just left Egypt. They had lived through years of suffering as slaves of the wicked king of Egypt. Then finally, Pharaoh had set them free. But wait! Pharaoh changed his mind and chased God's people to the edge of the Red Sea. They were trapped between the Red Sea and Pharaoh's soldiers. They needed help! What do you think happened?** Pause for responses.

Say: Moses prayed to God and asked for his help. And God answered Moses' prayer. God told Moses to raise his walking stick over the Red Sea. When he did, whoosh! The Red Sea split in half. God's people walked across on dry land. Then God caused the Red Sea to splash back together. The mean Egyptians were swept away. God helped Moses and the Israelites go free!

Let's make "Red Sea Salads" to remind us that God helps us. Then we'll discover how God helps us every day.

Have the children get into pairs, and hand each set of partners two paper cups and two plastic spoons. Following the directions on the recipe card, let each child make his or her own "Red Sea Salad." When everyone has finished preparing the salad, read aloud Exodus 14:16-22. Ask:

● **When has God helped you in a tough situation?**
● **Why does God help you?**
● **What are ways God sends help?**

Ask a child to pray for the class and thank God for his help. Then enjoy your "Red Sea Salads."

Extra Fun:

🖐 Play a game of Red Sea Tag. Place a long piece of masking tape down the center of the room as the Red Sea. Choose one child to be "Moses" to stand by the Red Sea. Instruct the other kids to stand about five feet away from the Red Sea on one side. When Moses says, "Cross the Red Sea by hopping," the kids must hop to the other side of the masking tape without being tagged by Moses. Whoever Moses tags may help tag others when Moses calls the kids across the sea again. Moses may call out various modes of travel, such as hopping on one foot, walking backward, or crawling.

🖐 Sing the following song to the tune of "Jesus Loves Me."

God helps me, this I know.	Yes, God helps me.
For the Bible tells me so.	Yes, God helps me.
He set Israel's people free,	Yes, God helps me.
Led them through the deep Red Sea.	He helps me all the time.

Water from a Rock
We can rely on God to give us what we need.

Water from a Rock
Serves 2

Theme to Remember: Trusting God
Verse to Devour: Exodus 17:6

Simple Supplies:

an orange

2 drinking straws

a plastic knife

2 resealable plastic sandwich bags

What to Do:

Rinse the orange; then cut it in half using the plastic knife. Place a half of the orange in each resealable plastic bag. Release the excess air and seal each bag. Make "water from a Rock" by squeezing the oranges. When you've squeezed all the orange juice out, open each bag slightly, and slide in a drinking straw. Sip and enjoy!

(From Group Publishing, Inc.'s *Incredible Edible Bible Fun*; copyright © 1997 Nanette Goings.)

The Message:

Set out oranges, plastic knives, drinking straws, and resealable plastic sandwich bags. Ask:

● Have you ever been really, really thirsty?
● What was it like?
● Who gave you a drink?

Say: The Bible tells us about a time when Moses and the Israelite people were very thirsty. The Israelites had lived in Egypt as Pharaoh's captives until God had freed them. God had parted the Red Sea, and Moses had led God's people out of Egypt. They were no longer slaves—but they *were* thirsty! For days they traveled in the hot desert, where there was plenty of sun and sand—but no water. The Israelites depended on God to give them what they needed, but how could they get water from sand and rocks? Moses prayed and trusted God. Then God told Moses to hit a rock with his walking stick. Moses did, and whoosh! Water came from the rock! What a miracle! The Israelites learned to trust God for their needs, and we can trust God to provide for us too.

Let's see if we can get something good to drink from pretend rocks. Then we'll learn more about trusting God.

Follow the directions on the recipe card. After everyone has squeezed "water" from the "rocks," read aloud Exodus 17:6. Ask:

● Do you think it was easy for the Israelites to trust God? Why or why not?

● Is it easy for us to trust God all the time? Explain.

● Does God always give you what you want? Why or why not?

● How can you trust God to provide for you this week?

Say: Moses trusted God when he led the Israelites in the desert. Moses trusted God when the people were thirsty. And God provided for them just as God provides for us.

Extra Fun:

☝ Young children especially will enjoy a rousing game of Rock, Rock, Water. Play the game like the age-old favorite Duck, Duck, Goose.

☝ Learn a rhyming prayer to repeat as you sip your "water" from the "rock."

Listen, God, I know you're there.

You heard Moses in his prayer.

I trust you, God, with all my heart,

And I know we'll never part. Amen.

Land-of-Milk-and-Honey Shake

God keeps his promises.

Land-of-Milk-and-Honey Shake

Serves 1

Theme to Remember: Keeping promises

Verse to Devour: Deuteronomy 26:15

Simple Supplies:

softened vanilla ice cream

milk

a spoon

a large paper cup

an ice-cream scoop

honey

a drinking straw

napkins

What to Do:

Place 1 scoop of vanilla ice cream in the paper cup. Fill the cup halfway with milk; then add 1 spoonful of honey. Stir and mix the ingredients with the spoon. Sip your "Land-of-Milk-and-Honey Shake" with a straw. Ahh...so cool and refreshing!

(From Group Publishing, Inc.'s *Incredible Edible Bible Fun*; copyright © 1997 Nanette Goings.)

The Message:

Set out vanilla ice cream, an ice-cream scoop, milk, honey, spoons, straws, large paper cups, and napkins. Gather children together, and ask:

● Have you ever waited for someone to keep a promise?

● What was it like to wait for that promise?

● Were you sure the promise would be kept? Explain.

Say: Waiting is often hard, and waiting for a special promise to be kept is one of the hardest things of all. Let me tell you about a special promise God made to his people, the Israelites. When you hear the word "promise," put your hand over your heart. After I've finished the story, I promise we'll make a delicious treat.

After the Israelites were set free from Egypt, they wandered in the desert. God promised them a land that was rich with milk and honey. What do you suppose God meant? Pause for responses. Then say: God promised the Israelites a land that was perfect for growing grain and for raising cattle and sheep. That was what the promise of milk and honey meant. But oh, the Israelites waited so long for God to keep his promise! Would he keep it?

Yes! The Israelites finally got to this wonderful land. They built homes, raised their children, and died in this land that God had promised them. God kept his promise to the Israelites just as he keeps his promises to us.

I promised you a delicious treat, and now I'll keep my promise, too. Let's make cool, refreshing "Land-of-Milk-and-Honey Shakes."

Following the directions on the recipe card, let each child make his or her own shake to enjoy. As the kids sip their cool treats, read aloud Deuteronomy 26:15. Then ask:

● Why do you think God made the Israelites wait so long to see the Promised Land of milk and honey?

● Do you think God's promises are worth waiting for? Explain.

● How do you trust God to keep his promises?

Close with the following prayer. Pray: **Dear God, we know we can always count on you to keep your promises. Help us to be patient and to wait for you to follow through in your time—not ours. Amen.**

Extra fun:

Sing this song to the tune of "Row, Row, Row Your Boat."

Go, go, go ahead

To the Promised Land.

Merrily, merrily, merrily, merrily

You are in God's hands.

Go, go, go ahead

To the Promised Land.

Merrily, merrily, merrily, merrily

God's promises will stand!

Send another class a note promising it a special treat. Then make "Land-of-Milk-and-Honey Shakes" for that class. Share with the class that God keeps his promises just as you kept your promise of a special treat!

Trumpet Treats
We can follow God's directions.

Trumpet Treats
Serves 6

Theme to Remember: Obeying God
Verse to Devour: Joshua 6:20

Simple Supplies:

grated Parmesan cheese

Cheerios

paper cups

Bugles

pretzel sticks

a paper lunch sack

measuring cups

What to Do:

Measure 2 cups of Bugles, 1/4 cup of grated Parmesan cheese, 1 cup of pretzel sticks, and 1 cup of Cheerios into a paper lunch sack. Close the bag, and then shake it to mix the ingredients. Serve your "Trumpet Treats" in paper cups, and share them with others. Crunch and munch!

(From Group Publishing, Inc.'s *Incredible Edible Bible Fun*; copyright © 1997 Nanette Goings.)

The Message:

Set out the Bugles, grated Parmesan cheese, pretzel sticks, Cheerios, paper grocery sacks, measuring cups, and paper cups.

Gather the kids together, and ask:

● Do you always obey the rules even when you don't understand the reasons behind the rules? Explain.

Say: It's not always easy to obey a teacher or a parent when we don't understand why we need to. And it's just as hard when God tells us to do something we don't understand. The Bible tells us about a time when God told Joshua, the Israelites' leader, to capture the city of Jericho in an unusual way. A tall wall went all the way around the city. God told Joshua to march with his army and seven priests around the city walls once a day for six days and to have the priests carry trumpets as they marched. Then God told Joshua that on the seventh day, they should march around the city seven times, blowing the trumpets; after the seventh time, the priests should blow the trumpets once more, and the people should shout loudly. Then the walls of Jericho would come down. Ask:

● How do you think Joshua felt when he heard God's plan?

Say: Joshua and his soldiers obeyed God, and everything happened just as God said it would! The walls came tumbling down, and the city of Jericho was captured by the Israelites.

Let's make crunchy "Trumpet Treats" to remind us that God tells us what to do.

Follow the directions on the recipe card. Let everyone help measure and shake the bags of crunchy treats. Then before the kids eat, read aloud Joshua 6:20. Ask:

● How can you know what God wants you to do?

● How can you obey God this week?

Close with the following prayer, and then let the kids gobble their goodies. Pray: **Dear God, you told Joshua what to do when he needed your help. Please help us listen to you and obey as Joshua did. Amen.**

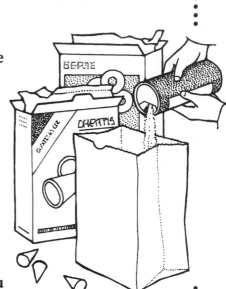

Extra Fun:

✋ Create your own "Joshua trumpets." Cut three-inch squares of wax paper. Using a rubber band, secure a piece of wax paper to one end of a cardboard tube. Hum through the open end of the tube as you would a kazoo. Create your own trumpet tunes, and have a concert.

✋ Invite half the class to sing the following song while the other half plays their Joshua trumpets. Sing the song to the tune of "Frère Jacques." Then switch singers' and trumpeters' roles.

> Are you sleeping,
> Are you sleeping,
> Jericho,
> Jericho?
> God's army marched around
> And blew a trumpet sound.
> Then the walls
> Tumbled down.

Strong-As-Samson Dip
Our gifts, talents, and abilities come from God.

Strong-As-Samson Dip
Serves 1

Theme to Remember: Gifts and talents
Verses to Devour: Judges 14:5-6

Simple Supplies:

mayonnaise

dry cream of spinach or

vegetable soup mix

a small paper cup

sour cream

measuring spoons

a plastic spoon

crackers

What to Do:

Measure 2 tablespoons of mayonnaise, 1 tablespoon of sour cream, and 1 teaspoon of cream of spinach or vegetable soup mix into a small paper cup. Stir the ingredients until they're thoroughly combined. Dip crackers into the "Strong-As-Samson Dip," and munch them down. Don't you feel stronger already?

(From Group Publishing, Inc.'s *Incredible Edible Bible Fun;* copyright © 1997 Nanette Goings.)

The Message:

Set out the mayonnaise, sour cream, soup mix, measuring spoons, paper cups, plastic spoons, and crackers. You may substitute raw vegetables for crackers if you choose.

Gather children together, and ask:

● **What special talent or gift do you have?** Allow children time to demonstrate their talents and special abilities.

● **Who do you think gave you special talents, gifts, and abilities?**

Say: Special talents and abilities are gifts that only God can give. And God has given each of us unique talents to use for his glory. The Bible tells us about a man named Samson who had a special gift from God—amazing strength! Samson could kill a lion with his bare hands. Now *that's* strong! But Samson didn't always use his strength for God's glory. In fact, Samson ended up in chains because he bragged about his gifts, and someone tried to stop him from using those gifts for God. How do you think God felt when Samson didn't use his gifts for God? Allow for responses.

In the end, Samson did use his awesome gift of strength for God. He pushed down the pillars that held up a temple and brought the temple crashing down on God's enemies! Yes, Samson was strong, but he realized that his strength came from God. And he used his special talent for God's glory.

Let's make "Strong-As-Samson Dip" to remind us that God gives us special gifts to use for his glory.

Help the kids make cups of the dip, following the directions on the recipe card. While everyone is enjoying crackers and dip, read aloud Judges 14:5-6. Then ask:

● In what ways can we use our gifts and talents?

● What gift or talent can you use for God this week?

Say: We all have special gifts and talents that God gave us. Let's remember to use them for God and to thank God for all he's given us.

Extra Fun:

Have some fun doing "Samson exercises" to build up your strength. Choose someone to be "Samson"; then have Samson lead the class in doing five repetitions of an exercise, such as jumping jacks, sit-ups, or five seconds of jogging in place. Then choose another person to be Samson. Continue until everyone has had a turn leading an exercise.

Invite kids to each create a coupon for their parents using one of their gifts or talents. The coupon could be redeemable for a colorful drawing, for ten minutes of reading aloud, or even for a "free" snack such as "Strong-As-Samson Dip" with crackers!

Gooey Grain Goodies

God wants us to be giving.

Gooey Grain Goodies
Serves 1

Theme to Remember:
Generosity and giving
Verses to Devour: Ruth 2:14-23

Simple Supplies:

z large marshmallows

crispy rice cereal

a paper plate

peanut butter

a plastic knife

napkins

What to Do:

Spread a small amount of peanut butter on the ends of z large marshmallows. Pour crispy rice cereal onto a paper plate. Roll the ends of the marshmallows in the cereal. Now you're ready to eat your "Gooey Grain Goodies!"

The Message:

Set out peanut butter, marshmallows, crispy rice cereal, plastic knives, napkins, and paper plates. You'll also need a bell and a small, covered container holding a few grains of dried rice to tell the Bible story.

Have children sit in a circle, and then ask:

● **Have you ever heard advertisements say, "This item can be yours—absolutely free"?**

● **What do you think when you hear these kinds of statements?**

Say: Claims for free things are often hard to believe. They make us want to ask, "What's the catch?" or "What do *I* have to do?" But if someone's heart is full of grace and true generosity, free gifts *can* be real!

Let's listen to a Bible story about a man named Boaz who gave a free gift to a woman named Ruth. You can help me tell the story. We'll pass around this container of rice and this bell. Each time you hear the word "grain," shake the container of rice if you're holding it. Each time you hear the name "Ruth," ring the bell if you're holding it. And finally, each time you hear the name "Boaz," everyone clap your hands. After you've held the grain or the bell, pass the item to the person sitting next to you. OK, let's start the story.

Say: <u>Ruth</u> and her mother-in-law, Naomi, were all alone. Their husbands had died. They decided to move to Bethlehem to be close to Naomi's relatives. Boaz was one of Naomi's relatives and owned a large field of delicious grain.

One day Ruth told her mother-in-law, "I'm going to go pick up the leftover grain in the farmers' fields. We can use the grain to make tasty bread." Ruth worked long and hard to gather the leftover grain. She happened to be working in Boaz's field.

Boaz saw Ruth working in the field and asked his servant, "Who's that hard-working woman?" The servant answered, "She is Naomi's daughter-in-law. Her name is Ruth." Boaz felt sorry for Ruth. He told his workers to leave extra grain in the field for Ruth to pick up. Then Boaz invited Ruth to eat with his workers. Boaz took care of Ruth and Naomi from that day on.

Say: Boaz generously offered Ruth a free gift of grain to help feed herself and Naomi. Let's make "Gooey Grain Goodies" to munch on. Then we'll learn more about being generous and giving to others.

Hand everyone a paper plate. Then help the kids follow the directions on the recipe card. After everyone has prepared two or three "Gooey Grain Goodies," set them aside. Read aloud Ruth 2:14-23, and then ask:

● Why was Boaz so generous with Ruth?

● Do you think that God wants us to be generous and giving with others? Explain.

● What are some ways you can be generous and giving this week?

Say: Boaz was generous when he gave extra grain to Ruth. He was generous when he invited Ruth to sit and eat with his workers. God wants us to be generous, too. Now let's say a prayer and ask God to show us how to give freely to others. Pray: Dear God, thank you for showing us your generosity. Please help us find new ways to give to others. Amen. Let kids enjoy their "Gooey Grain Goodies."

Extra fun:

🖐 Create your own "generosity coupons," and yes…they're really free! Coupons could include items such as "Good for one free room cleaning," "Good for setting the table tonight," "Good for one free back rub" or "Good for one big hug!"

🖐 Make extra "Gooey Grain Goodies" to generously give to members of the church staff or to an elderly or sick person in the congregation.

Baby's Bread

God wants us to serve him.

Baby's Bread
Serves 1

Theme to Remember: Serving God
Verses to Devour: 1 Samuel 1:10-11, 20-22

Simple Supplies:

2 slices of bread

a small jar of applesauce baby food

a spoon

softened cream cheese

a plastic knife

a paper plate

What to Do:

Spread softened cream cheese on 1 slice of bread. Then spread 1 spoonful of applesauce baby food over the cream cheese. Top the cream cheese and applesauce with a second slice of bread. Cut your "Baby's Bread" sandwich in half. Tastes good enough for any Samuel!

(From Group Publishing, Inc.'s *Incredible Edible Bible Fun;* copyright © 1997 Nanette Goings.)

The Message:

Set out bread, softened cream cheese, applesauce baby food, plastic knives and spoons, and paper plates. Ask:

● Have you ever given up something special? How did it feel?

● When is it important to give up something?

Say: It's not always easy to give things up—especially things that are very important to us. The Bible tells us about a woman named Hannah who made a tremendous sacrifice. She gave something very special to God.

Hannah prayed to God for a baby. She promised God that if he gave her a baby, she would give the baby back to God to serve him. Well God heard Hannah's prayers, and soon she had a baby. She named the baby Samuel. Hannah loved Samuel more than anything, but she also loved God. Hannah remembered her promise to God, so when Samuel was old enough, she took him to Eli the priest. Hannah loved her son, but she gave him up to serve God. Ask:

● Do you think Hannah was wise to give up Samuel? Why?

● What could you give up to serve God?

Say: Let's see if we can make our own "Baby's Bread" like Samuel might have eaten. Then we'll learn more about serving God.

Follow the directions on the recipe card. As everyone enjoys the "Baby's Bread," read aloud 1 Samuel 1:10-11, 20-22. Then ask:

● **How can you serve God at home? at school? at church?**

Say: **Hannah served God by keeping her promise to him. Let's look for ways we can serve God this week and always.**

⌶ Extra Fun:

☞ Serve God this week at church by straightening hymnals before the church service, sweeping the front sidewalk, or picking up trash on the church's property.

☞ Serve your mom or dad some "Baby's Bread" this week. Volunteer to make lunch and serve the special sandwiches with chips and a glass of cold milk.

Riverbed Stones

Faith in God is our strongest weapon against our fears.

Riverbed Stones

Serves 1

Theme to Remember: Faith in God
Verses to Devour: 1 Samuel 17:48-50

Simple Supplies:

1 stalk of celery

a plastic knife

small jelly beans or gumdrops

a paper towel

peanut butter

What to Do:

Rinse a celery stalk, and then pat it dry with a paper towel. Spread peanut butter down the center of the celery stalk. Now fill your "riverbed" with 5 smooth jelly bean or gumdrop "stones." Crunch 'n' munch away!

(From Group Publishing, Inc.'s *Incredible Edible Bible Fun;* copyright © 1997 Nanette Goings.)

The Message:

Set out celery, peanut butter, plastic knives, paper towels, and jelly beans or gumdrops. Say: **Do you know what the word "underdog" means? The dictionary says that an underdog is someone who is expected to lose in a contest.** Ask:

● **When have you felt like an underdog? What happened?**

Say: **The Bible tells us a story about a real underdog. His name was David, and he was a young shepherd. David volunteered to fight a giant bully named Goliath who stood over nine feet tall. Wow! Nine feet tall! Goliath was a soldier in an army that wanted to capture God's people and make them their slaves. David loved God and wanted to fight against mean Goliath.**

Goliath was ready for a battle. He wore a helmet and leg guards, had a coat of bronze armor that weighed more than a hundred pounds, and carried two huge spears and a sword. David had no spears. He had no armor. All he had was his sling and five stones. Who was the underdog? It seemed like David was, but David had the most powerful weapon of all—his faith in God! David knew that God would protect him no matter what. David shot one smooth stone from his sling, and guess what? It killed Goliath.

David overcame Goliath with one smooth stone from a riverbed—and lots of faith in God! Let's make delicious "Riverbed Stones" to remind us of the incredible story of David and Goliath. Then we'll talk more about faith.

Help kids follow the directions on the recipe card. After everyone has made a celery stalk of "Riverbed Stones," read aloud 1 Samuel 17:48-50. Then ask:

● Why wasn't David afraid of giant Goliath?

● How does our faith help us overcome fears in our lives?

● In what ways can you have more faith in God this week?

Say: Let's say a prayer and ask God to help us have more faith. Pray: Dear God, thank you for caring for us and for loving us in such great ways. Please help us have more faith and trust in you every day. Amen.

Let the children enjoy their "Riverbed Stones."

Extra Fun:

✋ Demonstrate how tall Goliath was in a fun way. Have kids lie head to toe on the floor and stretch, bend, or curl their bodies to measure exactly nine feet and four inches.

✋ Create your own "David slings" using plastic cups, string, and jingle bells or metal washers. Poke a hole in the bottom of each plastic cup. Thread an eighteen-inch piece of string through the hole, and knot the end so it doesn't pull through the cup. On the other end of the string, tie a jingle bell or metal washer. How many times can you get the "stone" into David's sling?

David's Snack-in-a-Snap

God protects us.

The Message:

Set out corn flakes, quick-cooking oats, the measuring cups, several large spoons, raisins, shelled sunflower seeds, resealable plastic bags, scissors, and dried apple slices.

Gather kids in a group, and ask:

● Have you ever been chased by someone in a game?

● How does it feel to know that someone's chasing you even in a game of Tag?

Say: The Bible tells us about a time David and his soldiers were being chased by a king named Saul. Saul didn't like David because God was going to make David the next king of Israel. King Saul wanted to kill David before he could be made king!

David had been hiding in caves and running from Saul for a long time. But God took care of David and protected him from King Saul's army. One time King Saul almost caught David, but a messenger came to tell King Saul to go to another part of the country. King Saul left right away, and David was safe! God protects and cares for us just as he cared for David.

Think about how fast David had to eat when Saul was chasing him! Let's make "David's Snack-in-a-Snap" to eat. Then we'll learn more about God's protection.

Help the children follow the directions on the recipe card to make individual snack bags. Then read aloud 1 Samuel 23:25-28. Ask:

● **Why do you think God protected David?**
● **When has God protected you?**

Close with the following prayer. Pray: **Dear God, you were with David his whole life, protecting and caring for him. Thank you for your protection in our lives today. Amen.**

Extra Fun:

👋 Play a fun game of Freeze Tag. To "unfreeze," name one way God protects you.

👋 Sing the following song as a prayer to God. Sing to the tune of "Jesus Loves Me."

God protects me, this I know.

For the Bible tells me so.

All of us to him belong.

We are weak, but he is strong.

Yes, God protects me.

Yes, God protects me.

Yes, God protects me.

The Bible tells me so.

Heavenly Bread
God gives us what we need.

The Message:

Set out the cake; plastic spoons, knives, and forks; nondairy whipped topping; paper plates; and the assorted toppings.

Gather children together, and ask:

● **When have you needed something? Who gave you what you needed?**

Say: **We often need things such as food, water, and new clothes. Usually the people who love us give us what we need if they can. There was a man in the Bible whose name was Elijah. And Elijah found out that God loves us enough to give us what we need, too. Elijah had no food and was very hungry and thirsty. He found a sparkling stream to drink from, but he was still hungry. Guess what God did? He sent a raven—a big, black bird—to bring meat and bread to Elijah. Think of it! A bird bringing bread from heaven! Elijah trusted God to give him what he needed, and we can trust God to give us what we need too.**

Let's make our own version of "Heavenly Bread" to eat. Then we'll discover how God provides for us.

Follow the directions on the recipe card. After everyone has decorated a slice of cake, read aloud 1 Kings 17:5-6. Then ask:

● How did Elijah know that God would give him what he needed?

● How does God provide for us?

Close with the following prayer. Pray: **Dear God, Elijah trusted you to give him what he needed. Help us trust you to provide what we need. And thank you for all that you give us. Amen.**

Let the kids enjoy their "Heavenly Bread"!

Extra Fun:

✋ Play a fun game of God Provides. Have the children form a circle. Start the game by naming one thing that God provides for you—for example, one friend. Then have the child to your right continue, naming your item first and then adding an item—for example, one friend and two trees. Continue around the circle, allowing each person a chance to list the previous items and add an item. How many things does God provide for you?

✋ Adapt this devotion, and use it when you're teaching about manna and about God's provision to Moses and the Israelites in the wilderness. Hide wrapped slices of the cake around the room, and then let the kids find the slices, bring them to a table, decorate them, and gobble them up.

Queen Esther's Crowns

God helps us be brave.

Queen Esther's Crowns
Serves 5

Theme to Remember: Bravery
Verses to Devour: Esther 2:14-16; 4:13-16

Simple Supplies:

a flour tortilla

strawberry jam

raisins

a paper plate

softened cream cheese

a banana

a plastic knife

What to Do:

Spread softened cream cheese on a flour tortilla. Then smooth strawberry jam on top of the cream cheese. Cut a banana into small pieces, and sprinkle the banana and raisins on top as the "jewels" in the "crown." Roll the tortilla, and slice the roll into 1-inch sections. Lay "Queen Esther's Crowns" cut-side down, and admire all of the "jewels" inside before munching.

(From Group Publishing, Inc.'s *Incredible Edible Bible Fun*; copyright © 1997 Nanette Goings.)

The Message:

Set out tortillas, softened cream cheese, strawberry jam, bananas, raisins, plastic knives, and paper plates.

Gather kids together, and say: **Turn to a partner, and tell him or her about one time when you needed to be brave.** Pause for kids to share with a partner. Then say: **Being brave isn't always easy, is it? The Bible tells us about a time a girl named Esther had to be very brave. Esther loved God, but she lived in a place where the king didn't love God at all.**

The king was looking for a new queen, and he chose Esther to be the queen. When her people's future depended on her, Esther gave her fears to God. God helped Esther be brave, and she saved God's people from destruction. God helped Esther be brave, and he'll help us be brave, too.

Let's make "Queen Esther's Crowns" to remind us that bravery comes from God. Then we'll talk about how God helps us be brave.

Help kids follow the directions on the recipe card. After everyone has made their "Queen Esther's Crowns," read aloud Esther 2:14-16; 4:13-16 or summarize the whole story. Then ask:

● **How did God help Queen Esther?**

● In what ways can God help you be brave?

● How does being brave help you serve God?

Say: Esther was brave because she knew that God loved her and would want her to stand up for his people. God helped Esther do a very hard thing, and God will help us do hard things, too.

⚡ Extra Fun:

🖐 Let kids create their own wearable, jeweled crowns. First make a headband from a brown paper grocery sack or construction paper. Then embellish the crown with glitter, plastic jewels, and sequins.

🖐 Teach kids a rhyming prayer that they can repeat the next time they need to be especially brave.

> Help me be brave, God.
>
> Help me be strong.
>
> Help me trust you, God,
>
> All the day long.
>
> Amen.

Daniel's Veggies

God wants us to be loyal to him.

Daniel's Veggies
Serves 1

Theme to Remember: Loyalty to God
Verses to Devour: Daniel 1:8, 12-17

Simple Supplies:

corn tortilla chips

a cherry tomato

a plastic fork

a paper plate

lettuce leaves

a plastic knife

grated cheddar cheese

spicy salsa or salad dressing (optional)

What to Do:

Place a handful of tortilla chips on a paper plate. Tear clean lettuce leaves into small pieces, and place them on the tortilla chips. Use the plastic knife to slice a cherry tomato into 4 pieces. Place the tomato pieces on the lettuce. Sprinkle grated cheddar cheese over your "Daniel's Veggies," and then top them with spicy salsa or salad dressing if you desire. Mmm, mmm, good—and so healthy, too!

(From Group Publishing, Inc.'s *Incredible Edible Bible Fun*; copyright © 1997 Nanette Goings.)

The Message:

Set out the tortilla chips, clean lettuce leaves, cherry tomatoes, plastic knives and forks, grated cheddar cheese, paper plates, and bottled salsa or salad dressing. Ask:

● What does it mean to be "loyal"?

● Who are you loyal to? Why?

Say: The Bible tells us about a man named Daniel who loved God and was very loyal to him. Daniel was taken as a slave to a king's palace in a foreign country. This king didn't know God or worship him. In fact, he worshiped false gods and wanted to teach Daniel and a few of Daniel's friends to do the same. How do you think Daniel felt? Allow kids to share their thoughts.

Say: Daniel and his friends loved God. They didn't want to worship the king's idols. And they didn't want to eat the king's meat, which had been offered to idols. They only wanted to serve God and worship him. What could they do? They decided to eat only vegetables and drink only water. Guess what happened! After ten days of eating vegetables and water, Daniel and his friends looked healthier than anyone else! Because of Daniel's love and loyalty to God, he soon became an important helper to the king.

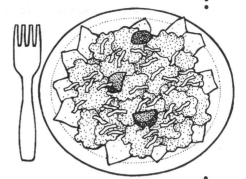

Let's make a special treat called "Daniel's Veggies." Then we'll learn more about being loyal to God.

Help kids follow the directions on the recipe card. While everyone is munching on "Daniel's Veggies," read aloud Daniel 1:8, 12-17. Then ask:

● **How did Daniel show loyalty to God?**

● **In what ways did God reward Daniel's loyalty?**

● **Why is being loyal to God important?**

Say: **In turn for Daniel's love and loyalty, God rewarded Daniel and his friends with great wisdom and the ability to learn many things. God will be good to us, too, when we love and obey him as Daniel did.**

Extra Fun:

☞ You may wish to serve "Daniel's Veggies" with "Tears-in-My-Eyes Salsa." The recipe is found on page 98.

Fiery Furnace Food

God watches over us and protects us all the time.

Fiery Furnace Food

Serves 1

Theme to Remember: God's protection
Verses to Devour: Daniel 3:26-27

Simple Supplies:

a graham cracker

3 small marshmallows

tiny cinnamon candies

aluminum foil

fudge sauce

a plastic spoon

What to Do:

Place a graham cracker on a large square of aluminum foil as the fiery furnace. Put the marshmallows on the graham cracker to represent Shadrach, Meshach, and Abednego; then drizzle fudge sauce over the marshmallows. Drop a few tiny cinnamon candies on top as flames. Fold the aluminum foil, and seal the edges around the cracker. Place the "fiery furnace" in a sunny spot for a few minutes or until the foil feels warm. Then unwrap the foil and enjoy your "Fiery Furnace Food."

(From Group Publishing, Inc.'s *Incredible Edible Bible Fun;* copyright © 1997 Nanette Goings.)

The Message:

Set out graham crackers, aluminum foil, small marshmallows, fudge sauce, tiny cinnamon candies, and plastic spoons. Ask:

● When does God watch over us?

● Why do you think God protects us all the time?

Say: God watches over us when we're at home, in school, and when we're afraid. In fact, God watches over us all the time. The Bible tells us about three friends who trusted God to watch over them. Shadrach (SHAYD-rak), Meshach (MEE-shack), and Abednego (a-BED-nee-go) served a king who wanted them to bow down and worship a false god. But the friends loved God and refused to worship the king's false god. That made the king very angry! In fact, he put all three friends in a fiery-hot furnace to get rid of them. What do you think happened? Allow time for children to respond. God sent an angel to protect them. The mean king learned that there is only one true god—our God! And just as God protected Shadrach, Meshach, and Abednego from the fiery furnace, God protects us all the time.

Let's make delicious "Fiery Furnace Food" to remind us of God's protection.

Follow the directions on the recipe card. While everyone's "fiery fur-

nace" is being warmed by the sun, read aloud
Daniel 3:26-27. Then ask:

● **How do you know that Shadrach, Meshach, and Abednego trusted God?**

● **How does God protect us?**

● **How can we trust in God's protection more?**

Share a prayer before eating the snack. Pray: **Dear God, thank you for watching over us. It's great to know that you're protecting us and keeping us safe all the time, wherever we are. Amen.**

Extra Fun:

Play this game and clean up your "cooking area" at the same time. After the kids have eaten their "fiery furnace food," have them crumple the aluminum foil into balls. Have them throw the shiny balls into the wastebasket, and say, "God watches over me when I...(ride in a car, take my dog for a walk, play with my sister)."

Play this "hot" guessing game to fill in extra moments.

I'm found in the kitchen.
I can be turned on.
I cook your food.
What am I? (A stove.)

I love to be outside.
I'm very hot and shining bright.
I come out by day and hide at night.
What am I? (The sun.)

I'm yummy to eat.
I look great in a bun.
I love to be gobbled up.
What am I? (A hot dog.)

Lion Chow

God wants us to pray to him.

The Message:

Set out the rice cereal squares, caramel syrup, powdered sugar, resealable plastic bags, measuring cups, and measuring spoons. Say: **Let's talk about lions!** Ask:

● **Where do lions live?**
● **What do lions like to do?**
● **What do lions like to eat?**

Say: **Did you know that we can read about lions in the Bible?**

One day, a mean king put a man named Daniel in a cave with hungry lions. You see, Daniel loved God and would only pray to God. Some people who didn't like God or Daniel convinced the king to make a law that people could pray only to the king. The king liked Daniel, but he couldn't go back on his law when he was told that Daniel had disobeyed the law and had prayed to God. So the king put Daniel in with the *hungry* lions to die. What do you think happened? God sent an angel to close the lions' mouths! Then the king understood God's power, and he told everyone to honor God! You see, not even a king's orders or hungry lions could stop Daniel from praying to God.

Let's make some crunchy "Lion Chow" to eat. Then we'll discover more about prayer.

Follow the directions on the recipe card, and let everyone make his or her own bag of "Lion Chow" to nibble. Then read aloud Daniel 6:19-23. Ask:

- **Why is it important to pray to God?**
- **How does prayer help us when we're in trouble?**
- **How can you draw closer to God in prayer this week?**

Say: Daniel refused to pray to anyone but God. That's because he loved God and knew that prayer helps us stay close to God. It's important to know that God wants us to pray to him, and we can pray to God every day!

Extra Fun:

☞ Make a lion's mask from a large paper grocery sack. Slip the sack over your head, and mark where the eyes will go. Then remove the sack, and cut out holes for the eyes. Add construction paper fringe for the mane, and use a marker to draw on whiskers and other facial features. Become pretend lions to act out the story of Daniel in the lions' den.

Whale of a Sandwich

God wants us to obey him.

Whale of a Sandwich
Serves 1

Theme to Remember: Obedience
Verses to Devour: Jonah 3:2-3

Simple Supplies:

a can of tuna

a tablespoon

a paper cup

a plastic spoon

a can opener

mayonnaise

2 saltine crackers

a slice of bread

What to Do:

Open the can of tuna, and drain the liquid. Put 2 tablespoons of tuna and 1 tablespoon of mayonnaise into the paper cup. Crush 2 small crackers into the paper cup. Stir the crumbs into the tuna-and-mayonnaise mixture. Spread the tuna salad on half a slice of bread; then fold the other half of the bread over to make a sandwich. For extra fun, use a fish-shaped cookie cutter to cut the bread. What a fine snack you've "fished up!"

(From Group Publishing, Inc.'s *Incredible Edible Bible Fun*; copyright © 1997 Nanette Goings.)

The Message:

Set out the canned tuna, a can opener, tablespoons, mayonnaise, paper cups, saltine crackers, plastic spoons, and bread. For extra fun, use a fish-shaped cookie cutter to cut the bread.

Say: **Sometimes our parents or teachers want us to do things we really don't want to do. Tell about a time when that's happened to you.** Encourage children to respond.

Say: **The Bible tells us about a man named Jonah. When God asked Jonah to go to a city called Nineveh to tell people about him, Jonah refused. He didn't like the people of Nineveh because they were mean. Jonah tried to run away by hopping on a boat. But God sent a storm, and Jonah was sorry he hadn't obeyed God. Jonah ended up being thrown into the sea, but God sent a *big* fish to swallow him. Jonah spent three days inside the fish and prayed for forgiveness. God made the big fish spit Jonah out onto land. And guess what? Jonah obeyed God and went straight to the city of Nineveh!**

Let's make delicious sandwiches to remind us how important it is to obey God.

Help the kids follow the directions on the recipe card. After everyone has made a sandwich, read aloud Jonah 3:2-3. Then ask:

● What did Jonah learn when he didn't obey God?

● Should we always obey everyone? Explain.

● Why is obeying God sometimes difficult?

● How can you obey God this week?

Say: Jonah thought he knew what was best for him. He didn't want to obey God. But God had another plan for Jonah and saved his life so that he could ask forgiveness and obey God again. We need to remember to obey God in all that we do, too.

Let the kids enjoy nibbling their sandwiches.

Extra Fun:

Sing a song about Jonah to the tune of "London Bridge."

Jonah, go to Nineveh,

Nineveh, Nineveh.

Jonah, go to Nineveh.

Do what God says!

Jonah went the other way,

Other way, other way.

Jonah went the other way,

Poor, poor Jonah.

Jonah learned to obey God,

Obey God, obey God.

Jonah learned to obey God.

We should too!

Spicy Stars

We can celebrate Jesus' birth any time!

Spicy Stars
Serves 1

Theme to Remember:
Celebrating Jesus' birth
Verses to Devour: Matthew 2:10-11

Simple Supplies:

5 gingersnap cookies

a teaspoon

creamy peanut butter

star-shaped cookie cutters

sugar

a resealable plastic sandwich bag

corn syrup

wax paper

cinnamon

napkins

What to Do:

Place 5 gingersnap cookies in a resealable plastic bag, and seal it. Crush the cookies into fine crumbs. Open the bag to add 2 teaspoons of corn syrup and 1 teaspoon of creamy peanut butter. Close the bag, and knead the ingredients until a dough forms. Remove the dough from the bag, and flatten it on a square of wax paper. Cut out star shapes, and then sprinkle the dough cookies with cinnamon and sugar.

(From Group Publishing, Inc.'s *Incredible Edible Bible Fun;* copyright © 1997 Nanette Goings.)

The Message:

Set out gingersnap cookies, resealable plastic bags, teaspoons, corn syrup, peanut butter, wax paper, star-shaped cookie cutters, cinnamon, sugar, and napkins. Ask:

● Have you ever received an invitation to a special party?

● How did you feel about going to the special party?

Say: Special parties are fun! Let me tell you about a special "party" and how three wise men were invited. At the time of Jesus' birth, God put a bright star in the sky for the wise men to follow. They followed the star for many weeks until it came to rest over the place where Jesus, Mary, and Joseph were staying. Thanks to the star, the wise men found the baby King! They knelt down to worship Jesus and gave him gifts of gold, frankincense, and myrrh. Frankincense and myrrh were expensive spices and very special gifts. But Jesus was a special baby, and the wise men wanted to celebrate his birth.

Let's make some delicious "Spicy Stars" to remind us how the wise men celebrated Jesus' birth. Then we'll celebrate Jesus' birth together.

Help kids follow the directions on the recipe card. If the dough is sticky, add another crushed gingersnap. If the dough is too dry, add another teaspoon of corn syrup.

After everyone has cut out and spiced up several stars, read aloud Matthew 2:10-11. Then ask the following questions:

● **How did the wise men celebrate Jesus' birth?**

● **How did their gifts show love?**

● **How can we celebrate Jesus' birth today?**

Close by singing the following song to the tune of "Twinkle, Twinkle, Little Star."

> **Twinkle, twinkle, little star.**
> **What a super sign you are.**
> **Up above the world so high,**
> **Announcing Jesus in the sky.**
> **Twinkle, twinkle, little star.**
> **You helped the wise men travel far.**

Extra fun:

🖐 Young children will enjoy acting out the story of the three wise men. Encourage the children to join in the actions at the end of each sentence.

The wise men traveled many weeks. Their camels' feet went stamp, stamp, stamp.

The wise men followed a distant star. Their eyes went blink, blink, blink.

The wise men found baby Jesus. Their mouths went ooh, ooh, ahh.

The wise men bowed to worship him. Their knees went creak, creak, creak.

The wise men gave their precious gifts. Their hearts went thump, thump, thump.

🖐 Play a fun game of Star Search by hiding paper stars throughout the room and by having the kids hunt for them.

Locusts-and-Wild-Honey Bites

We can be ready for Jesus.

Locusts-and-Wild-Honey Bites

Serves 1

Theme to Remember:
Preparing for Jesus

Verses to Devour: Matthew 3:1-4

Simple Supplies:

measuring spoons

nonfat powdered milk

an 8-ounce paper cup

peanut butter

honey

a plastic spoon

What to Do:

Measure 2 tablespoons of peanut butter, 2 tablespoons of nonfat powdered milk, and 1/2 teaspoon of honey into a paper cup. Stir until a dough forms. Add a bit more nonfat powdered milk if the dough is too sticky. Knead the dough with your clean hands. Then use the dough to "sculpt" pretend bugs and locusts. Enjoy your "wild honey bites" and share some with a friend.

(From Group Publishing, Inc.'s *Incredible Edible Bible Fun*; copyright © 1997 Nanette Goings.)

The Message:

Set out peanut butter, nonfat powdered milk, honey, paper cups, measuring spoons, and plastic spoons.

Gather kids in a group, and say: **I have a fun rhyming story to tell you about someone who wanted people to get ready for Jesus. The man's name was John, and God had told John to tell people that Jesus was coming into the world. John, or John the Baptist as many called him, ate very strange food. Listen to the story to find out what John ate.**

The Bible tells of John, a man who loved God.

He lived a kind of life that people thought odd.

His clothes were made of camel hair.

He lived in the desert—but *what* could grow there?

He ate bugs called locusts and lots of wild honey.

John didn't mind, though others thought it funny.

John was to tell about Jesus, you see.

For Jesus was coming to love you and me.

"Be ready for Jesus; prepare now the way,

For Jesus is coming! That's what I say!"

John wanted us all to be ready for Jesus,

For he knew God's Son would love us and free us.

Say: That's the rhyming story about John the Baptist and how he told people to get ready for Jesus. Now what did John like to eat? Let the children tell that John ate locusts and wild honey.

Say: Let's make our own "Locusts-and-Wild-Honey Bites." They'll sure taste better than what John ate! Then we'll talk about how to be ready for Jesus.

Follow the directions on the recipe card. While everyone is sculpting and nibbling their dough, read aloud Matthew 3:1-4. Then ask:

● Why was John the Baptist's job important?

● Why do you think it's important to be ready for Jesus?

● How can we make sure we're preparing for Jesus?

Say: John the Baptist told people that Jesus was coming. John knew how important it is to be ready to accept Jesus into our lives. And we can prepare our hearts to be nearer Jesus, too.

Extra Fun:

John prepared the people for Jesus' coming. Help young children understand that preparing for something means getting ready. Let children prepare a surprise party for another class. Have them hang balloons around the room and tape crepe paper to chairs and doorways. Invite children to make extra "Locusts-and-Wild-Honey Bites" for the other class. Then invite the children from the other class to come to a surprise party. Be sure to have your children explain about preparing for Jesus.

Foolish Houses

God wants us to obey his Word.

Foolish Houses
Serves 1

Theme to Remember: Obedience
Verses to Devour: Matthew 7:24-27

Simple Supplies:

a graham cracker

cold milk

a tablespoon

a plastic spoon

instant chocolate-pudding mix

a paper cup

a resealable plastic bag

What to Do:

Spoon 1 tablespoon of instant chocolate-pudding mix and 3 tablespoons of cold milk into a paper cup. Stir until the ingredients are mixed. Break a large graham cracker into 4 sections. Place 3 sections inside the resealable plastic bag. Crush the graham cracker sections into fine crumbs, or "sand." Sprinkle the sand over the chocolate pudding in the cup. Place the remaining graham cracker "house" in the sand. Gobble your house before it sinks into the sand!

(From Group Publishing, Inc.'s *Incredible Edible Bible Fun*; copyright © 1997 Nanette Goings.)

The Message:

Set out instant chocolate-pudding mix, cold milk, graham crackers, resealable plastic bags, paper cups, plastic spoons, and tablespoons. Ask:

● What does the word "foolish" mean?

● When have you acted foolishly?

● What would have been the wise thing to do instead?

Say: **Jesus tells a story in the Bible about a wise man and a foolish man. The wise man built his house on solid rock, but the foolish man built his house on sand.** Ask:

● **What do you think happened when the rain fell down and the flood waters came up?** Encourage children to share their ideas.

Then say: **The foolish man's house was washed away, but the wise man's house stood firmly.**

Jesus told this story to teach us about building our lives on the right foundation. When we build our lives on the solid rock of Jesus, we stand firm when life's problems come along. But if we center our lives on flimsy things, such as money or possessions, we'll fall flat when troubles arise. Jesus warns that when we don't listen to God's Word and obey it, we're like the foolish man whose house was washed away. But when we listen to God's Word and obey it, we're like the wise man who built his house on solid rock.

Let's build our own "Foolish Houses" to remind us of Jesus' story. Then we'll discover more about obeying God's Word.

Follow the directions on the recipe card. When everyone has made a "Foolish House" to eat, read aloud Matthew 7:24-27. Then ask:

● Why is it wise to obey God's Word?
● How can we learn to obey God more?

Close with the following prayer. Pray: **Dear God,** thank you for giving us the Bible to show us how to obey you. Please help people who have built their lives on "sand" learn to obey you. And help us keep our lives on you as our solid rock. Amen.

Extra Fun:

✍ Create your own "solid rock" paperweights. Select smooth, medium-sized rocks, and use permanent markers or paint pens to decorate them. Be sure to include a Scripture reference to Matthew 7:24-27 on the rocks.

✍ Sing the following song to the tune of "Old MacDonald Had a Farm."

Old Man Foolish built a home,	Old Man Wisdom built a home,
E, I, E, I, O.	E, I, E, I, O.
And to that home, there came a storm,	And to that home, there came a storm,
E, I, E, I, O.	E, I, E, I, O.
With a crash, crash here and a smash, smash there,	With a creak, creak here and a groan, groan there,
Here a crash, there a smash,	Here a creak, there a groan,
Everywhere a crash, smash.	Everywhere a creak, groan.
Old Man Foolish had no home,	Old Man Wisdom still had his home,
E, I, E, I, O.	E, I, E, I, O.

Seed Sandwiches

God wants his Word to grow in our lives.

Seed Sandwiches
Serves 1

Theme to Remember:
Understanding God's Word
Verses to Devour: Matthew 13:3-8

Simple Supplies:

a slice of bread

sesame seeds or hulled sunflower seeds

a paper plate

softened cream cheese

a plastic knife

What to Do:

Spread softened cream cheese on a slice of bread. Sprinkle the slice freely with sesame seeds or hulled sunflower seeds. Fold over the piece of bread to make a sandwich, and nibble your sandwich as the birds nibbled the seeds in Jesus' parable of the sower and the seeds. These sandwiches can also be toasted in a toaster oven for a different flavor—but ask an adult to help you do this!

(From Group Publishing, Inc.'s *Incredible Edible Bible Fun*; copyright © 1997 Nanette Goings.)

The Message:

Set out bread, softened cream cheese, sesame seeds or hulled sunflower seeds, plastic knives, and paper plates. You'll also need a few, small paper-scrap "seeds" for each child, several sesame seeds or sunflower seeds, and a small container of dirt.

Gather children together, and say: **Let's imagine that we're farmers. In the spring, we plant crops in the field. Here are some pretend seeds.** Hand each child several paper seeds. **Let's plant the seeds.** Toss the paper seeds into the air. Then say: **What do you think happened to the seeds we planted? Let's see. Some of the seeds fell on the road. Birds swooped down and ate the seeds. Those seeds didn't grow.** Have children pretend to be crows and make "cawing" sounds as each child picks up one or two paper seeds.

Say: **Some of the seeds fell among thorns and stones. Those seeds choked and withered, and their roots couldn't live. Those seeds didn't grow either!** Have each child pick up a few more paper seeds.

Say: **But some of the seeds fell in good soil. And with warm sunshine and plenty of water, they grew strong and tall. The plants produced a good crop and seeds that could be planted to produce even more!**

Jesus told this story to teach us that we should accept his teachings and let them grow in our lives just as the good dirt accepted the seeds and let them grow. As we let God work in our lives, we'll produce the kind of fruit he wants us to produce just as the seeds that fell in the good soil did.

Let's make "Seed Sandwiches" to remind us to let God's Word grow and produce good fruit in us.

Follow the directions on the recipe card. When everyone has prepared a seed sandwich to munch, read aloud Matthew 13:3-8. Then ask:

● Is it always easy to understand and obey God's Word? Explain.

● Why are Jesus' teachings important in our lives?

● How can we let Jesus' words and teachings "grow" in us this week?

Say: Let's always try to understand God's Word and let it grow in our lives.

Extra Fun:

🖐 Learn more about trusting God and his Word by demonstrating a "faith fall." Have a child stand with his or her back to you. Encourage the child to fall backward; then catch him or her. Explain that faith in God is like a free fall—we trust God and his Word and know he'll be there to catch us when we have troubles.

🖐 Learn a fun clapping rhyme to repeat with a partner.

Seeds by the road,
They don't grow.
Seeds in the rocks,
Wouldn't you know?
Seeds in the thorns,
Ouch! Oh! Oh!
But seeds in the good soil,
Watch them grow!

Fish and Chips
Jesus provides for us.

The Message:

Set out resealable plastic bags; a box of fish-shaped crackers; and an assortment of the following munchies: gummy fish, cereal loops, chocolate chips, raisins, marshmallows, oyster crackers, raisins, and popcorn.

Gather kids in a group, and ask:

● What's it like to be really, *really* hungry?

● How would you feed a huge crowd of hungry people?

Say: The Bible tells us about a time when Jesus fed a huge crowd. In fact, there were more than five thousand people! Where do you suppose he got enough food to feed that many hungry mouths and tummies? Pause for responses. Then say: **Jesus had been teaching the huge crowd about God, and it was late in the day. Everyone was very hungry, but there was no food except for what a little boy had in his lunch: five small loaves of bread and two fish. That was it! But Jesus provided for those hungry people. He blessed the bread and fish and then fed all the people. They even had leftovers! Jesus showed everyone that he provides what we need—sometimes in very miraculous ways!**

Let's prepare bags of "Fish and Chips" to remind us how Jesus fed five thousand people with five loaves of bread and two fish. Then we'll discover how Jesus provides for us.

Follow the directions on the recipe card. While the kids munch their "Fish and Chips," read aloud Matthew 14:18-21. Then ask:

● **How does Jesus provide for us?**
● **Why do you think Jesus sends people who help care for us?**
● **Who can you help care for this week?**

Close with the following prayer. Pray: **Dear Lord, thank you for providing good food to eat, nice homes to live in, and families to help care for us. Let us help you by helping others this week. Amen.**

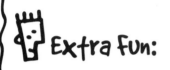 **Extra Fun:**

✋ Add a variation to the "Fish and Chips" devotion. Let children form pairs and then help their partners prepare their bags of "Fish and Chips." Encourage partners to thank each other for their thoughtful help.

✋ Young children will enjoy doing this finger rhyme before munching their "Fish and Chips."

Jesus cares for me. *(Point to yourself.)*

He loves me, can't you see? *(Hug yourself.)*

My parents, friends, and teachers, too *(clap for each person named)*,

All help Jesus—yes, they do! *(Nod your head "yes.")*

Mighty-Mustard-Seed Sauce

God helps us do great things when we have faith in him.

Mighty-Mustard-Seed Sauce
Serves 1

Theme to Remember:
Trusting in God
Verse to Devour: Matthew 17:20

Simple Supplies:

mayonnaise

pretzels or raw, cleaned vegetables

a plastic spoon

prepared mustard

a 4-ounce paper cup

measuring spoons

What to Do:

Measure 2 tablespoons of mayonnaise and 1/2 teaspoon of prepared mustard into a paper cup. Stir the mayonnaise and mustard until it's completely mixed. Dip pretzels or raw vegetables into the "Mighty-Mustard-Seed Sauce" for a mighty yummy snack!

(From Group Publishing, Inc.'s *Incredible Edible Bible Fun*; copyright © 1997 Nanette Goings.)

The Message:

Before class, you'll need a mustard seed for each child in class. Mustard seeds are available in the spice section of most grocery stores.

Set out mayonnaise, prepared mustard, paper cups, pretzels, plastic spoons, and measuring spoons. You may also want to set out raw, cleaned vegetables.

Hand each child a mustard seed. Ask:

● **Do you know what kind of seed this is?**

Say: **You're holding mustard seeds, and although they look tiny, they're really powerful little seeds! If you plant your mustard seed, it will burst through the ground and shoot up into a tree taller than a grown-up. Isn't that amazing? Jesus said something surprising about a mustard seed to help us understand that we can accomplish great and mighty things through our faith in God.**

Did you know that the mustard we eat on hot dogs and sandwiches is made from mustard seeds? We can use mustard to make a delicious treat called "Mighty-Mustard-Seed Sauce." It will remind us that we can do great things with God's help.

Follow the directions on the recipe card. When everyone has mixed his or her own cup of mustard sauce, read aloud Matthew 17:20. Then ask:

● How much faith is faith the size of a mustard seed?

● What "mountains," or troublesome things in our lives, can God take care of if we have faith in him?

● Through your faith in God, what might he help you accomplish during this week? during your lifetime?

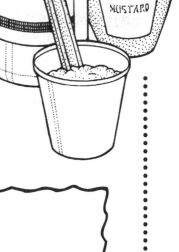

Say the following prayer to close. Pray: **Dear God, thank you for telling us about the mustard seed in the Bible. Just like a tiny mustard seed, we can grow strong in our faith and can accomplish many great things with your help. Amen.**

Let the kids enjoy dipping pretzels and raw vegetables into the mustard sauce.

Extra Fun:

✋ Plant the mustard seeds in small pots or in a sunny, outdoor garden. Remember to water the sprouts often as they grow.

✋ Pretend to be a growing mustard seed. Roll into a tiny ball, then begin to stretch out into a "seedling." Slowly stand as your reach your "leaves" toward the warm sun. Stand on your tiptoes as you become a tall, strong "mustard tree."

Handle-With-Care Fudge
Jesus loves children.

Handle-With-Care Fudge
Serves 1

Theme to Remember: Love
Verses to Devour: Matthew 19:13-14

Simple Supplies:

a chocolate graham cracker

a teaspoon

napkins

chocolate syrup

a resealable plastic sandwich bag

What to Do:

Place 1 whole chocolate graham cracker inside a resealable plastic bag. Release the excess air; then seal the bag. Crush the graham cracker into fine crumbs with your hands. Open the bag, and add 2 teaspoons of chocolate syrup. Seal the bag. "Handle with care" as you knead the ingredients in the bag until they form a ball of "fudge." Open the bag, and enjoy your "Handle-With-Care Fudge."

(From Group Publishing, Inc.'s *Incredible Edible Bible Fun*; copyright © 1997 Nanette Goings.)

The Message:

Set out chocolate graham crackers, chocolate syrup, teaspoons, resealable plastic bags, and napkins.

Ask children:

● What does the phrase "handle with care" mean?

● What do you think could be inside a box marked, "Handle With Care"?

Say: When something needs to be handled with care, it needs to be treated very carefully, as if it's valuable and breakable. The Bible tells about a time when Jesus told his followers about someone who was very important to him and who needed to be handled with care. Jesus told the disciples how carefully children should be treated. He made children feel welcome and loved. Jesus even said adults need to have faith like a child has! Jesus knows how precious kids are and wants children to be handled with care.

We can make "Handle-With-Care Fudge," and then we'll talk about Jesus' love for each of us.

Follow the directions on the recipe card. When everyone has made a bag of fudge, read aloud Matthew 19:13-14. Ask:

● Why did Jesus want children to come to him?

● How can you handle others with care this week?

Say: **We're all important to Jesus, and he especially loves children. Let's say a prayer of thanks for Jesus' love.** Pray: **Dear Lord, thank you for loving us. And thank you for letting us know how precious children are to you. We love you, too. Amen.**

Extra Fun:

🖐 Show your love for others by creating your own "handle-with-care first-aid kit" to give a friend. Place a plastic bandage, a cotton ball, a wrapped towelette, a tissue, and a peppermint candy inside a plastic sandwich bag.

🖐 Play a fun game of carefully, carefully on a hot summer day. Have each child take a turn carrying on his or her head a paper cup filled halfway with water. Have each child walk down the sidewalk and back, transferring the cup to the next child in line for his or her turn. If a child spills, refill the cup. Point out that "handle with care" means treating something or someone very carefully and lovingly.

Vineyard Grapes

God is just and fair.

Vineyard Grapes
Serves 1

Theme to Remember: Fairness
Verses to Devour: Matthew 20:1-16

Simple Supplies:

grapes

a resealable plastic sandwich bag

paper towels

fruit-flavored gelatin mix

a teaspoon

What to Do:

Wash the grapes, and remove them from the stem. Place 10 to 12 damp grapes in the resealable bag. Put 2 teaspoons of fruit-flavored gelatin mix into the bag. Seal the bag, and then shake it until all the grapes are coated with gelatin. Open the bag, and nibble your "Vineyard Grapes." For a frosty treat, place the coated grapes in the freezer for a few hours before nibbling them.

The Message:

Set out grapes, fruit-flavored gelatin mix, paper towels, teaspoons, and resealable plastic bags.

Gather children together, and say: **Raise your hand if you've ever said, "She has more than I have!"** Pause. **Put your finger on your nose if you've ever said, "It was my turn!"** Pause. **Tap your head if you've ever said, "That's not fair!"** Pause. **Sometimes when we think we've been treated unfairly, we complain and grump and mope around. But we can be sure that God is always fair.**

Jesus told a parable about workers in a vineyard—the place where grapes are grown—who thought they weren't being treated fairly. All of the vineyard workers were paid the same amount even though some worked the entire day and others worked only an hour. Ask:

● **How would you feel if you got a dollar for working all day and someone else got a dollar for one hour of work?**

● **Would it be fair? Explain.**

● **What if you had agreed in advance to work all day for a dollar?**

Say: **What might look fair or unfair to us might not be what is fair or unfair to God. It's the same with getting to heaven. We don't get to heaven by doing lots of good things. Whoever has a** relationship with God through Jesus will go to heaven.

God is fair to all of us and wants us to be fair to each other. I'll be fair and give you each ten grapes. Then we'll prepare "Vineyard Grapes" to nibble and munch as we learn more about fairness.

Follow the directions on the recipe card. While everyone is enjoying the grapes, read aloud Matthew 20:1-16. Then ask:

● Why does God want us to be fair?

● How can you be fair to others this week?

Close with the following prayer. Pray: **Dear God,** sometimes it's hard to be fair. Help us remember that you treat us fairly and justly. And help us be fair with friends and family this week. Amen.

Extra Fun:

✋ Enjoy this great grape craft. Let kids put on paint shirts and then use grape juice or purple paint to create pictures of grapes. Use the grape stems from your treats as crazy paintbrushes. When the pictures are dry, add details using markers.

✋ Play Group of Grapes when the kids want a challenge. Have the kids stand in a circle and reach across to hold the hand of someone on the opposite side of the circle. Then have kids hold the hand of another person with their free hands. The circle has now turned into a cluster of tangled grapes. Let the kids work together to untangle the "grapes" without letting go of each other's hands.

Fluttery Butterflies
Jesus is alive!

Fluttery Butterflies
Serves 1

Theme to Remember:
Jesus' resurrection

Verses to Devour: Matthew 28:5-6

Simple Supplies:

a can of pineapple slices

a small paper plate

string cheese

candy sprinkles

a can opener

a plastic knife

a whole maraschino cherry

What to Do:

Open the can of pineapple slices, and drain the juice. Place 1 pineapple ring on a paper plate. Slice the pineapple ring in half, and turn the halves to make 2 curved butterfly wings. Unwrap the string cheese, and cut it in half. Place half of the string cheese between the wings as the butterfly's body. Use a whole maraschino cherry as the butterfly's head. Decorate the wings with candy sprinkles. Eat and enjoy!

(From Group Publishing, Inc.'s *Incredible Edible Bible Fun*; copyright © 1997 Nanette Goings.)

The Message:

Set out cans of pineapple rings, a can opener, string cheese, maraschino cherries, plastic knives, candy sprinkles, and paper plates.

Gather children together, and say: **I have a riddle for you. See if you can guess what springtime insect I am.**

My pretty wings flutter from hour to hour.
I flitter and fly to every flower.
What am I?

Say: That's right—a butterfly! The butterfly sometimes reminds us of Easter and of the new life we have in Jesus. The butterfly begins life as a caterpillar and then makes a cocoon and stays inside for several weeks. It seems as though the caterpillar has died, but when it comes out of the cocoon, it's changed into a beautiful butterfly that flies into the sky!

Jesus died on the cross, and his body was placed in a tomb, which is a little like a cocoon. And three days later, Jesus rose from the dead and came out of the tomb—like a butterfly emerging from its dark cocoon. And we know that Jesus is alive and with us today!

Let's make delicious "Fluttery Butterflies" to celebrate that Jesus is alive!

Follow the directions on the recipe card. After everyone has made a "Fluttery Butterfly," read aloud Matthew 28:5-6.

Ask:

● **What does it mean to us that Jesus is alive today?**

As kids are enjoying their treats, say: **Whenever we see a butterfly in the spring, it reminds us that Jesus is alive and with us today!**

Extra Fun:

✋ Create your own fuzzy caterpillars by gluing yarn pompoms on craft sticks. Place adhesive-backed magnet strips on the backs of the caterpillars, and use them as refrigerator magnets.

✋ Create your own "flying" butterflies. Tear out a colorful page from a magazine or catalog. Accordion-fold the paper; then tape around the center to make the butterfly's body. Bend a pipe cleaner for antennae, and tape it to the body of the butterfly. Tape long pieces of thread to the centers of the butterflies; then suspend the butterflies from the ceiling or a window, and watch them flutter!

Three-in-One Cinnamon Snack

God the Father, the Son, and the Holy Spirit loves us.

Three-in-One Cinnamon Snack

Theme to Remember: The Trinity

Serves 1

Verses to Devour: Matthew 28:18-20

Simple Supplies:

a slice of bread

a plastic knife

cinnamon-sugar (Make cinnamon-sugar
   by combining 1 tablespoon of sugar
   and 1/2 teaspoon of cinnamon.)

a paper plate

softened margarine

What to Do:

Spread softened margarine on one side of the slice of bread. Sprinkle the cinnamon-sugar mixture over the margarine. Cut the bread into 4 triangle-shaped pieces by cutting diagonally from corner to corner in an X shape. The triangles remind us of the Trinity. The bread, margarine, and cinnamon-sugar remind us that God, the Son, and the Spirit are three in one and one in three.

(From Group Publishing, Inc.'s *Incredible Edible Bible Fun;* copyright © 1997 Nanette Goings.)

The Message:

Set out the bread, paper plates, plastic knives, softened margarine, and cinnamon-sugar.

Say: **Let's look around the room for triangles. How many triangles can you see?** Pause for children to respond.

Say: **Sometimes God is referred to as the Trinity because God is three persons—the Father, the Son, and the Holy Spirit—in one being. A triangle is sometimes used to symbolize the Trinity because it is one shape but has three points. Like the three points of a triangle, God is three in one: the Father, Jesus, and the Holy Spirit.**

Let's make "Three-in-One Cinnamon Snacks" to remind us of the Trinity.

Follow the directions on the recipe card. As you prepare the sandwiches, say: **These snacks are three things in one, kind of like the Trinity.** Then explain each ingredient as follows:

As you place the bread on the plate, say: **God is like this piece of bread. He is the one who made us and who gives us life.**

As you spread the margarine, say: **Jesus is God's Son who spread his love to all of us and died for our sins so we could someday go to heaven.**

As you sprinkle on the cinnamon-sugar, say: **The Holy Spirit is like** this cinnamon-sugar. When the Holy Spirit is sprinkled throughout our lives, we're able to do things that God wants us to do.

As you cut the bread into triangles, say: **Each triangle has three points and reminds us of the three parts of the Trinity: the Father, the Son, and the Holy Spirit.**

After you've made the sandwiches, read aloud Matthew 28:18-20. Then ask:

● **How can you tell others about the Father, Jesus, or the Holy Spirit this week?**

Say: **God the Father, Son, and Holy Spirit continually works in our lives to help our faith grow. We can thank God for all he's done for us and tell others about how wonderful he is!**

🖐 Extra Fun:

🖐 Take a walk together outside and look for triangle shapes to remind you of the Trinity. As you spot each triangle, touch the points and tell the names of the three members of the Trinity.

🖐 Create "Trinity triangles" pictures or a classroom poster. Cut colorful construction paper triangle shapes, and glue them to a large sheet of paper or a length of shelf paper. Title your pictures or poster "God: the Three in One!"

Kisses from God

Jesus is God's gift of love to us.

Kisses from God
Serves 1

Theme to Remember: God's love
Verses to Devour: Luke 2:7; John 3:16

Simple Supplies:

an 8-ounce paper cup

softened margarine

wax paper

3 wrapped chocolate-kiss candies

a plastic spoon

corn syrup

powdered sugar

measuring spoons

What to Do:

Place 1 tablespoon of softened margarine and 2 teaspoons of corn syrup in a paper cup. Add powdered sugar until the cup is about half full. Stir gently; then spoon the dough onto wax paper. Add powdered sugar if the dough is too sticky or margarine if it's too dry. Knead the dough until it's soft; then form 3 small dough balls. Flatten the dough balls with your palms. Unwrap 3 candy kisses, and place 1 in the middle of each dough circle. Wrap up the kisses with the dough like Mary wrapped up baby Jesus in a blanket.

(From Group Publishing, Inc.'s *Incredible Edible Bible Fun*; copyright © 1997 Nanette Goings.)

The Message:

Set out paper cups, plastic spoons, softened margarine, corn syrup, powdered sugar, wax paper, measuring spoons, and chocolate-kiss candies. Ask the kids:

● **What's the most special gift you've been given?**

● **How is giving a gift a special way to show love?**

Say: **God loves us so much that he gave us a very special gift. Who is God's gift of love?** Let children tell that Jesus is a gift of love from God.

Say: **That's right! God gave us Jesus. In fact, it's almost like he gave us a kiss of love when he gave us his Son. What a special gift! God even sent angels to announce his gift of love.** Hold up one of the chocolate-kiss candies. Say: **And to make sure this first Christmas gift was even more special, Jesus' mother, Mary, gift-wrapped Jesus. She lovingly wrapped Jesus in soft cloth and laid him in a manger. God loved the world so much that he gave us a special kiss from heaven—Jesus!**

Let's wrap up some special "Kisses From God."

Following the directions on the recipe card, let each child wrap two or three "kisses" with their dough. As they enjoy the sweet treats, read aloud Luke 2:7 and John 3:16. Then ask:

● How did God show his love for us when he sent Jesus?

● How can you thank God this week for his precious gift of Jesus?

Say: Every time you wrap a present during the Christmas season, remember that the best present of all was from God. Jesus was God's special gift of love to us!

Extra Fun:

👋 Play this fun version of Hide-and-Seek. Wrap a chocolate kiss in a four-foot strip of crepe paper to make a "gift ball." Tape the end of the strip to the ball. Make one gift ball for each member of the class. Then hide the gift balls throughout the room before children arrive. Let the children look for their special hidden gifts.

👋 Make this quick craft with chocolate-kiss candies to remind kids that angels announced Jesus' birth. Twist a two-inch section of gold pipe cleaner into the shape of a halo. Poke the end of the halo into the top of the wrapped candy kiss. Glue white paper or doily "wings" to the back of the candy kiss. Finally, tie a loop of thread around the halo, and hang your chocolate-kiss "angel" on a Christmas tree.

Good News Mouths

We can tell others about God.

Good News Mouths
Serves 1

Theme to Remember:
Telling others about God
Verses to Devour: Luke 5:9-11

Simple Supplies:

half an apple

marshmallow creme or peanut butter

a plastic knife

4 small marshmallows

What to Do:

Clean the seeds from the apple half. Cut the apple half in half lengthwise again to make two smiling lips. Spread marshmallow creme or peanut butter on the white portions of the apple pieces. Place 4 marshmallow "teeth" on the peanut butter or marshmallow creme. Then stack the apple halves on top of each other to make a mouth. Yum! Yum!

(From Group Publishing, Inc.'s *Incredible Edible Bible Fun*; copyright © 1997 Nanette Goings.)

The Message:

Set out apple halves, plastic knives, marshmallow creme or peanut butter, and marshmallows. Ask:

● Have you ever had really big news and didn't know how to tell everyone?

Say: The Bible tells us about a time when Jesus chose special helpers to help him tell others about God. Jesus met two brothers who were fishermen. Their names were Simon Peter and Andrew. Jesus asked them to go with him to be fishers of people. Then he met two brothers named James and John and asked them to be special helpers, too. Soon Jesus had twelve helpers or disciples. And the disciples helped Jesus tell people the truth about God.

Let's make yummy "Good News Mouths." Then we'll discover how we can tell others about God.

Follow the directions on the recipe card. When everyone has made a "Good News Mouth," read aloud Luke 5:9-11. Then ask:

● Why did Jesus choose the twelve disciples?

● What does it mean to "fish for people"?

● How can you be a disciple this week and tell others about God?

Say: Jesus had twelve disciples who helped him tell others about

God. They were Jesus' "fishers of people." And we can be fishers of people by telling others about God too.

Extra Fun:

Create your own "disciple pompoms" to help tell others about Jesus. Hand each child three three-foot crepe paper streamers. Have the kids fold their streamers in half; then staple or tape them in the center to make pompoms. Let kids use them to shout the following cheer:

Jesus, Jesus—he's the one!

Jesus, Jesus—he's God's Son!

Jesus died to save us all,

And he wants us to heed his call!

"Good Fruit" Fruit Salad
We draw others to Jesus by the way we treat them.

"Good Fruit" Fruit Salad
Serves 1

Theme to Remember: Modeling Jesus' love

Verses to Devour: Luke 6:43–45

Simple Supplies:

lemon-flavored drink mix

a plastic spoon

a variety of fruit including seedless

   grapes, strawberries, banana slices,

   pineapple chunks, maraschino cherries, or

   mandarin orange slices

lemon-lime soda pop

an 8-ounce paper cup

a 1/8-cup measuring cup

What to Do:
Fill an 8-ounce paper cup halfway with fruit. Sprinkle a spoonful of lemon-flavored drink mix over the fruit. Pour 1/8 cup of lemon-lime soda pop over the fruit. Watch your " 'Good Fruit' Fruit Salad" bubble with joy; then enjoy its wonderful flavor!

(From Group Publishing, Inc.'s *Incredible Edible Bible Fun;* copyright © 1997 Nanette Goings.)

The Message:

Set out fruit, lemon-flavored drink mix, lemon-lime soda pop, measuring cups, plastic spoons, and 8-ounce paper cups. You'll also need two bananas. Refrigerate one banana until the peel turns brown.

Gather kids and ask:

● What does it mean to be or to set a good example for someone?

● Who are people you know who set good examples?

Say: Jesus told many stories, or parables, using everyday, common items. If Jesus were telling a story to our class today, he might just use these two bananas to tell a parable. Hold up both bananas. Ask:

● Which one of these bananas would you like to eat? Why?

Say: Jesus told a story to people about good and bad fruit. He taught that a good tree doesn't produce bad fruit, nor does a bad tree produce good fruit. Jesus wanted us to know that people who are truly good bring *good* things out of their hearts to share with others. By our good examples, we help others to know and love Jesus.

Peel the skin from the brown banana. Give a piece of the peel to each child. Then say: When we tell others about Jesus, they can change on the inside and become his "good fruit," too.

Let's make " 'Good Fruit' Fruit Salad" to remind us to be known

by the good things we say and do.

Help the kids follow the directions on the recipe card. When everyone has finished, read aloud Luke 6:43-45. Then ask the following questions:

● **What does it mean to be "good fruit" for Jesus?**

● **Why is it important to be a good example?**

● **How can you be a good example to kids who are unkind?**

Close with the following prayer. Pray: **Dear God, help us be your good fruit and share that fruit with others. Amen.**

🖐 Extra Fun:

🖐 Play a fun game of Mirrored Examples. Have children get into pairs and stand or sit facing their partners. In each pair, have one partner pretend to look into a mirror and move his or her arms and legs while the partner mirrors the actions. Then have partners switch roles.

🖐 Play this "mysterious" guessing game as you enjoy your " 'Good Fruit' Fruit Salads."

God made me a *long* fruit.
He made me yellow.
God made me very "a-peel-ing" to monkeys and kids.
What am I? (A banana.)

God made me a sweet fruit.
He made me red with a little, green cap.
God covered me with little, tiny seeds.
What am I? (A strawberry.)

God made me a round, little fruit.
He made me green or red or purple.
God made me to grow on a vine.
What am I? (A grape.)

God made me a juicy fruit.
He made my name the same as my color.
God made me with bumpy skin.
What am I? (An orange.)

Stormy-Sea Shake

Jesus is with us when we're afraid.

Stormy-Sea Shake
Serves 1

Theme to Remember: Jesus' protection
Verses to Devour: Luke 8:22-25

Simple Supplies:

blueberry yogurt

a ripe banana

a plastic knife

a resealable plastic sandwich bag

milk

a 1/4-cup measuring cup

a drinking straw

What to Do:

Measure 1/4 cup of blueberry yogurt and 1/4 cup of milk into the resealable bag. Cut off 1/4 of the ripe banana, and add it to the bag. Release the excess air from the bag, and then seal it tightly. Shake, squish, and mix your own "stormy sea." When the ingredients are thoroughly mixed, open the bag slightly, and slide in a drinking straw. Sip and enjoy!

(From Group Publishing, Inc.'s *Incredible Edible Bible Fun;* copyright © 1997 Nanette Goings.)

The Message:

Set out blueberry yogurt, milk, ripe bananas, drinking straws, measuring cups, plastic knives, and resealable plastic bags.

Gather the children together, and ask:

● **What makes you afraid?**

● **Who helps you deal with your fears?**

Say: **The Bible tells about a time Jesus' disciples were very afraid. You can help review the story. When you hear the word "waves," rock back and forth. When you hear the word "wind," blow to make windy sounds. Ready?**

Jesus and his disciples were sailing one night in the middle of a lake. Suddenly, a crashing storm hit! There was thunder and lightning and lots of <u>wind</u>. The boat was tossed up and down on the <u>waves</u>. The disciples were sure they'd drown in that stormy sea. Over the roar of the <u>wind</u> and the <u>waves</u>, the disciples asked Jesus to help them. And when Jesus raised his arms and told the storm to stop, the <u>wind</u> stopped blowing, and the <u>waves</u> became calm. The disciples learned that Jesus was more powerful than anyone or anything—and that Jesus helps us when we're afraid.

Let's make delicious "Stormy-Sea Shakes" to sip. Then we'll talk about how Jesus calms our fears.

Help the kids follow the directions on the recipe card. While everyone sips a "Stormy-Sea Shake," read aloud Luke 8:22-25. Ask:

● Why did Jesus help the disciples by calming their fears?

● How do we know that Jesus is with us when we're afraid?

● What can you do if you're afraid this week?

Say: Just as Jesus was with his disciples when they were afraid, Jesus is with us when we're afraid. It's important to remember that Jesus is *always* with us!

Extra Fun:

Young children will enjoy singing this song to the tune of "Row, Row, Row Your Boat." Encourage children to row pretend boats as they sing.

Row, row, row your boat
Gently out to sea.
Merrily, merrily, merrily, merrily,
Stormy clouds I see.

Row, row, row your boat
Gently out to sea.
Merrily, merrily, merrily, merrily,
Jesus is with me!

Reenact the Bible story from Luke 8 with a large pan of water and a toy boat. Make "stormy seas" by blowing across the water. For fun sight and sound effects, dim the lights, and let children use aluminum pie pans for crashing thunder and flashlights for lightning.

Good-Sam Gruel

Jesus wants us to be kind to others.

Good-Sam Gruel
Serves 1

Theme to Remember: Kindness
Verses to Devour: Luke 10:25-37

Simple Supplies:

instant rice

Cinnamon-sugar (Make your own
   Cinnamon-sugar by mixing
   1 tablespoon of sugar with
   1/2 teaspoon of Cinnamon.)

an 8-ounce foam cup

raisins

hot water

a plastic spoon

a 1/4-cup measuring cup

What to Do:
   Measure 1/4 cup of hot tap water into the foam cup. Add 1/4 cup of instant rice. Stir in raisins and Cinnamon-sugar to taste. Stir the mixture; then let it sit for 5 minutes. "Good-Sam Gruel" must surely be healthy, and it tastes so good, too!

(From Group Publishing, Inc.'s *Incredible Edible Bible Fun*; copyright © 1997 Nanette Goings.)

The Message:

Set out instant rice, hot water, raisins, cinnamon-sugar, foam cups, measuring cups, and plastic spoons. You'll also need a bandage.

Hold up the bandage, and ask:

● What is a bandage used for?

● Who can help others when they're hurt or need attention?

Say: Jesus wants us to know that we can help others who need us. To teach that, Jesus told a story about some people who didn't help and one who did! Let's listen to the story rhyme.

Long, long ago in a land far away,
A man walked down a road one day
When up from behind him, who should appear
But rough, mean robbers causing hurt and fear.
The poor man was beaten and was left for dead.
Two men walked by—"We'll not help him," they said.
They ignored the man though he was in pain.
"Why should we help him? What would we gain?"
Then a man from Samaria came along.
He cared for the man until the man was strong.
Now tell me, who was caring, loving, and kind?

The first two men acted like they were blind.
But the good Samaritan did what he could;
He cared for the man when no one else would!

Say: Even though the two men who passed by could have stopped to help the hurt man, they didn't. But just as Jesus would have helped, the good Samaritan helped the hurt man. We can be like the good Samaritan and help those who need our help.

Let's help each other make a yummy treat called "Good-Sam Gruel." Then we'll talk more about how we can be kind to others.

Follow the directions on the recipe card. Encourage children to help each other by holding each other's cups as they stir their gruel. While the gruel sits for five minutes, read aloud Luke 10:25-37. Then ask:

● Who does Jesus want us to be kind to?
● Is it easy to be kind to everyone? Explain.
● How can you be kind to someone this week?

Say: Just as the good Samaritan was kind to the hurt man, Jesus wants us to be kind to others. We can show others that we love Jesus by showing kindness to everyone.

Extra Fun:

✋ Invite kids to brainstorm about ways to show kindness and generosity in church or school. Suggest ways such as letting someone else be first in line, offering someone else the biggest piece of cake, or taking the last turn. Give each child a plastic bandage to put around a finger to help remind him or her to be kind to others.

✋ Say this prayer before eating your "Good-Sam Gruel." Let half of the children say the first part of each sentence while the other half finishes each sentence with, "Help me to be kind." Then have the kids switch roles.

Dear God, when others are mean,
Help me to be kind.
When others are sad,

Help me to be kind.
When others are hurting,
Help me to be kind.
Amen.

Pods and Peanuts

God loves us even when we do wrong.

Pods and Peanuts
Serves 1

Theme to Remember: forgiveness
Verses to Devour: Luke 15:11-24

Simple Supplies:

peanuts in the shell

a rolling pin

honey

a plastic knife

a resealable plastic sandwich bag

softened margarine

measuring spoons

crackers

What to Do:

Shell 10 peanuts, and place the nuts in the resealable plastic bag. Release the excess air from the plastic bag, and then seal the bag tightly. Crush the peanuts using the rolling pin. Then open the bag, and add 1/2 teaspoon of softened margarine and 1/4 teaspoon of honey. Seal the bag, and squeeze together the ingredients inside until they form a lump of "peanut butter." Open the bag, and use the plastic knife to spread your treat on crackers. Then eat!

(From Group Publishing, Inc.'s *Incredible Edible Bible Fun;* copyright © 1997 Nanette Goings.)

The Message:

Set out peanuts in the shell, softened margarine, honey, resealable plastic bags, rolling pins, measuring spoons, plastic knives, and crackers.

Gather the kids together, and ask:

● When have you needed to apologize? How did you feel?

Say: Jesus once told a story about a farmer who had two sons. The younger son asked his father for a huge amount of money. The father gave his son the money, and immediately the son went to the city and spent all his money foolishly. He had no money left for clothes or a place to stay. He couldn't even afford food! He got a job feeding pigs, and was so hungry that he ate the pigs' food. The young man decided to go home and ask his father for a job as a servant. Well, do you know what? The father welcomed his son back and gave him food to eat and new clothes to wear. The father forgave his son, and most of all, he still loved his son.

Say: Jesus told this story to teach us that God is like the loving, forgiving father in the story. Even when we do wrong, God loves us and forgives us when we're sorry.

Let's make a delicious treat called "Pods and Peanuts." Then we can discover more about God's forgiveness.

Help the kids follow the directions on the recipe card, and then read aloud Luke 15:11-24. Ask:

● **How can we be more forgiving of others?**

● **How can we ask God's forgiveness for wrong things we've said and done?**

Say: **The son in this story might have had to eat peanut shells when he was without money for food. But God is our heavenly Father. He loves and forgives us even when we do wrong things. And he gives us good things like our peanut butter snacks!**

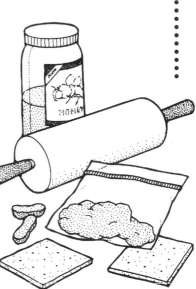

Extra Fun:

✋ Play a forgiveness game using the peanut shells left from the snack. Lay sheets of newspaper on the floor. Give each person a couple of peanut shells, and challenge him or her to think of one or two things for which they need forgiveness. Have kids stomp the shells on the newspaper while saying, "God loves you and forgives you." Point out that when God forgives us, he doesn't remember our wrongs any more.

It's Alive! Bread

Jesus came back to life on the third day.

It's Alive! Bread
Makes 1 loaf

Theme to Remember: Patience
Verses to Devour: Luke 24:6-7

Simple Supplies:
For the starter, you'll need...a small resealable plastic bag, a 1/4-cup measuring cup, flour, milk at room temperature, a 1/2-teaspoon measuring spoon, yeast

To complete the bread, you'll need...1/2 cup of water, 1/2 cup of "It's Alive! Bread" starter, 1 tablespoon of cooking oil, 1/2 teaspoon of salt, 2 cups of flour, 1 teaspoon of yeast, a spoon, a large bowl, a greased loaf pan

What to Do: Put 1/4 cup of flour, 1/4 cup of milk, and 1/2 teaspoon of yeast into the resealable plastic bag. Seal the bag, and shake it until the ingredients are well-mixed. Set the bag aside for 3 days without refrigerating it. Be sure to release air from the bag frequently.

After 3 days, mix together the rest of the ingredients in a large bowl. Knead the dough for about 5 minutes, and then place it into a greased loaf pan. Let the dough rise for 15 minutes, and then bake it at 350 degrees for 15 to 20 minutes.

(From Group Publishing, Inc.'s *Incredible Edible Bible Fun;* copyright © 1997 Nanette Goings.)

The Message:

Set out the supplies for the "It's Alive! Bread" starter: measuring cups and spoons, milk at room temperature, flour, yeast, and resealable plastic bags. Ask the kids:

● What special events have you counted down the days waiting for?

● How fast does time seem to pass when we're waiting for one of those special events?

Say: **Sometimes waiting is hard. The Bible tells us that when Jesus' friends put his body in the tomb, they were sad because they loved Jesus. But on the third day Jesus rose from the dead just as he had told them he would. He was with his friends again! He was alive! Their waiting was over!**

We're going to make "It's Alive! Bread" starter. The bread will come to life after a while, but you'll have to wait three days before you can make it into a loaf of bread.

Follow the directions on the recipe card. While kids are mixing the ingredients for the starter in their bags, read aloud Luke 24:6-7. Then ask:

● When was the last time you had to wait for something?

● What would you have said if you had seen Jesus alive on that first Easter morning?

● **What can you do in the next three days to tell others about Jesus?**

Have kids take home their bags of bread starter and the recipe for making the "It's Alive! Bread." Encourage kids to look at the bread starter at least once a day to watch it come to life.

Note: This recipe is intended to be completed at home with the help of a parent after three days. You may want to call parents to encourage them to help children bake the bread and to discuss the miracle and significance of Jesus' resurrection three days after his death.

Extra fun:

👋 Have the kids act out the following action verse.

Jesus is alive today (clap with each syllable)

As I jump and run and play! (Jump with each word.)

Jesus is alive today! (clap with each syllable.)

Hip-hip, hip-hip, hip-hooray! (cheer, jump, and be ecstatic!)

👋 Take the kids outside for a walk. Have them look around for things that are alive. Even in the winter or in the city, you'll find many of God's living creations.

Miracle Water
Jesus can do anything.

Miracle Water
Serves 1

Theme to Remember: Jesus' miracles
Verses to Devour: John 2:7-10

Simple Supplies:

a lemon

a resealable plastic sandwich bag

a 1/2-cup measuring cup

sugar

a plastic knife

water

a tablespoon

a drinking straw

What to Do:

Rinse a lemon; then cut it in fourths using the plastic knife. Place 1 piece of lemon in the resealable plastic bag. Seal the bag, and then squeeze the lemon inside the bag until all the juice is squeezed out. Open the bag, and add 1/2 cup of water and 1 tablespoon of sugar. Seal the bag tightly, and shake it until the sugar has dissolved. Open the bag slightly, and poke in a drinking straw. Sip and say "ahh!"

(From Group Publishing, Inc.'s *Incredible Edible Bible Fun;* copyright © 1997 Nanette Goings.)

The Message:

Set out lemons, water, sugar, resealable plastic bags, plastic knives, measuring cups and spoons, and drinking straws. Before class, cut a small slice of lemon for each child.

Hold up a lemon, and ask:

● **What fruit am I holding?**
● **How do lemons taste?**

Say: **Today I brought a slice of lemon for each of you to taste.** Give each child a lemon slice, and encourage children to taste the fruit. Say: **Lemons are very sour, aren't they? But did you know that we can change sour lemons into something sweet? In a little while, we'll find out how. But first I have a story to tell you about a time Jesus did something *very* amazing. Jesus and his mother, Mary, went to a wedding in a town called Cana. There were a lot of people there, and the people were enjoying delicious refreshments until the wine ran out. Mary asked Jesus to help, and Jesus told the servants to fill large jars with water from the well. Then Jesus changed that plain water to good wine! In fact, the host said it was the sweetest wine that had been served at the party! It was Jesus' first miracle, but he performed many amazing miracles in the years after that.**

We can't do miracles like Jesus can. But we can turn sour lemons into sweet treats.

Help the kids follow the directions on the recipe card. When everyone has made "Miracle Water" to sip, read aloud John 2:7-10. Then ask:

● **Why do you think Jesus changed water into wine?**

● **Why does it strengthen our faith to know that Jesus can do anything?**

● **How can you rely on Jesus' strength in your life?**

Close with the following prayer. Pray: **Dear God, we know that only you perform miracles, and we thank you for your wonderful actions. Help us recognize the miracles you perform to help us in our lives every day and to show us your great love. Amen.**

Extra Fun:

Play a memory game of What's Changed? Place a row of objects in front of the class; then have children close their eyes. Quietly remove one of the objects. Tell children to open their eyes and guess what changed in the row of objects. For older children, add more objects and remove two or three at a time. Invite children to take turns being the "Remover."

Invite young children to sing the following action song to the tune of "Frère Jacques."

It's amazing! It's amazing! (Hold your arms up high.)

God's own Son is the one. (Point upward, and then hold up one finger.)

Jesus can do anything. Jesus can do anything. (Clap in rhythm.)

He's God's Son! He's God's Son! (Point upward.)

Living Water

Jesus is with us when we're lonely.

Living Water
Serves 1

Theme to Remember: Loneliness
Verses to Devour: John 4:13-14

Simple Supplies:

a tablespoon

powdered milk

instant vanilla-pudding mix

a 1/2-cup measuring cup

a drinking straw

a teaspoon

orange-flavored drink mix

a resealable plastic sandwich bag

water

What to Do:

Measure 1 tablespoon of powdered milk, 1 tablespoon of orange-flavored drink mix, and 2 teaspoons of instant vanilla-pudding mix into a resealable plastic bag. Seal the bag, and shake it to mix the ingredients. Open the bag, and add 1/2 cup of cold water. Release the excess air; then seal the bag tightly. Shake the bag for several seconds. Then open one corner of the bag, and slide in a drinking straw. Sip and enjoy!

(From Group Publishing, Inc.'s *Incredible Edible Bible Fun*; copyright © 1997 Nanette Goings.)

The Message:

Set out powdered milk, orange-flavored drink mix, instant vanilla-pudding mix, water, resealable plastic bags, drinking straws, and measuring cups and spoons.

Gather the children together, and ask:

● When have you felt lonely?

● How did you get over feeling lonely?

Say: It's no fun to feel lonely, but we've all felt that way at one time or another. The Bible tells us a story about a woman in Samaria who was very lonely. In Jesus' time, people didn't have faucets or sinks to get water from. So every day, the women visited the town well for water. The well was also a place where women met friends and chatted about their families. Now, the lonely woman didn't have friends to meet at the well or a family to care for. The other women didn't like her. They wouldn't even *talk* to her!

One day Jesus stopped at the well. Guess who was there? The lonely woman. In that day, men didn't talk to strange women, and Jews like Jesus didn't talk to Samaritans. But Jesus asked the woman for a drink. She was shocked! This man was talking to her! Didn't he know that she was from Samaria? Jesus told her that he could give her more than plain water from a well; he could give her "living water" that gave life to the spirit. He also told her who he was. The woman was amazed and ran to tell others about Jesus. When Jesus lives in us, we never have to feel lonely again! Let's make our own version of "Living Water."

Help the kids follow the directions on the recipe card. When everyone has finished mixing their orange drinks, read aloud John 4:13-14. Ask:

● In what ways did Jesus help the woman?
● What did Jesus mean by "living water"?
● How can Jesus help you when you're lonely?

Say: Just as Jesus gave the Samaritan woman living water so she'd never have to be lonely, Jesus can give each of us that living water. We never need to be lonely as long as we have Jesus living in us.

Extra fun:

🖐 Sing this Bible song to the tune of "The Farmer in the Dell."

The woman at the well.	The woman at the well.
The woman at the well.	The woman at the well.
Jesus, she is all alone.	Jesus, you love everyone.
The woman at the well.	The woman at the well.
The woman at the well.	The woman at the well.
The woman at the well.	The woman at the well.
Jesus, she needs a friend.	Jesus, she will spread the news.
The woman at the well.	The woman at the well.

🖐 Play a fun, outdoor game of Living Water. Fill a spray bottle with water, and hand it to a child you've chosen to be "It." Have the rest of the children run around until It says "freeze." The children must stay frozen until the "living water" is squirted onto one of their hands.

Bubblin'-Pool Drink

Jesus can do anything.

Bubblin'-Pool Drink
Serves 1

Theme to Remember: Jesus' miracles
Verses to Devour: John 5:8-9

Simple Supplies:

prepared lemon-lime soft drink

a maraschino cherry with its stem

a teaspoon

blue powdered gelatin

a clear plastic drinking cup

What to Do:

Fill the drinking cup almost full with lemon-lime soft drink. Add 1/2 teaspoon of blue powdered gelatin to the soft drink. Watch your drink turn into a "pool" of sparkling, blue bubbles! Float a cherry in the pool for a colorful touch. Sip and savor!

(From Group Publishing, Inc.'s *Incredible Edible Bible Fun*; copyright © 1997 Nanette Goings.)

The Message:

Set out a pitcher of prepared lemon-lime soft drink, blue powdered gelatin, clear plastic drinking cups, maraschino cherries, and teaspoons.

Ask:

● When have you thought you could do something but found out you really couldn't?

● Is there anyone who really can do anything? Explain.

Say: Lots of times, we think we might be able to do something but find out we can't. Maybe we think we can lift a heavy package, or maybe we want to make someone feel better but don't know how. That's why it's important to know that Jesus can do anything!

The Bible tells about a time Jesus came to a pool in the Temple area. Many sick people came to the pool to rest. Some of the people were blind, and some of them couldn't walk. Once in a while, the pool would start to bubble and move. The people believed that the first person to get into the moving water would be healed.

One man, who had been sick for thirty-eight years, was lying by the side of the pool. He couldn't walk and couldn't get into the bubbling pool by himself. Jesus asked the man if he really wanted to be well. The man said "yes!" Then Jesus told the man to stand up and walk. And guess what happened? Pause for children to tell their ideas. Then say: **The man walked! Jesus had performed a miracle! And everyone learned that Jesus can do anything!**

Let's make our own delicious "Bubblin'-Pool Drinks." Then we'll learn more about Jesus' miracles.

Help the kids follow the directions on the recipe card. When everyone has made "Bubblin'-Pool Drinks" to sip, read aloud John 5:8-9. Then ask:

● **Why do you think Jesus performed miracles?**

● **How are miracles a way that Jesus shows his love?**

● **What great things has Jesus done in your life?**

Say: **Jesus can do anything. In the Bible, we can read of times he calmed stormy seas, turned water to wine, made blind people see, and even raised people from death. Only Jesus is a miracle-maker, and only Jesus can do anything.**

Extra Fun:

☞ Watch a "miracle" take place before your eyes. Let kids plant fast-growing marigold seeds. With water and sunshine, your "miracle marigolds" will sprout and grow.

Marvelous Mud

Jesus heals us.

Marvelous Mud

Serves 1

Theme to Remember: Jesus' healing
Verses to Devour: John 9:1–11

Simple Supplies:

instant chocolate-pudding mix

a 1/2-cup measuring cup

a resealable plastic sandwich bag

a tablespoon

cold milk

a drinking straw or a plastic spoon

What to Do:

Measure and pour 3 tablespoons of instant chocolate-pudding mix into the resealable plastic bag. Add 1/2 cup of icy-cold milk. Release the excess air from the bag; then seal it tightly. Shake and gently squish the ingredients to completely mix your chocolaty "mud." Open the bag slightly, and poke in a drinking straw or a plastic spoon. Sip or scoop your edible mud and enjoy!

(From Group Publishing, Inc.'s *Incredible Edible Bible Fun*; copyright © 1997 Nanette Goings.)

The Message:

Set out the instant chocolate-pudding mix, cold milk, resealable plastic bags, measuring cups and spoons, and drinking straws or plastic spoons.

Gather kids in a group, and ask:

● **What do you get when you mix dirt and water?**

Say: **You get mud! Now mud doesn't seem very special. In fact, mud is made from ordinary dirt and water. But Jesus used ordinary things to help heal people. He even used mud! Let me tell you that story. Each time you hear the word "mud," rub your hands together and say, "Ooey-gooey mud!" Ready?**

One day Jesus saw a man who had been born blind. People asked Jesus if the man was blind as a punishment for being bad. Jesus said no, that the man was blind so that God's wondrous healing power could be shown. Then guess what Jesus did? He made <u>mud</u>! Jesus scooped up dirt, spit on it, and mixed it into <u>mud</u>. Then he put the <u>mud</u> on the blind man's eyes. Now don't try this at home; after all, only *Jesus* can do anything! Jesus told the man to wash the <u>mud</u> from his eyes. And when the man did, he could see! Jesus gave the man his sight.

Now let's make edible "Marvelous Mud" to remind us that Jesus has the power to heal and help us.

Help the kids follow the directions on the recipe card. When everyone has finished mixing the "Marvelous Mud," read aloud John 9:1-11. Then ask:

● **Why do you think Jesus healed the blind man?**

● **How does Jesus heal our hearts and minds as well as our bodies?**

Say: **Jesus performed many miracles in his life, and his miracles helped and healed people. We know that Jesus can heal us, too. Let's thank Jesus for his healing power. Pray: Dear Lord, thank you for your power, which can heal hearts, minds, and bodies. We love you. Amen.**

Extra Fun:

✋ Create your own edible "mud paintings." Mix up a bowl of chocolate pudding. Place one to two tablespoons of chocolate pudding on a paper plate, and finger-paint with clean fingers. Licking this special "mud" off your fingers is as fun as painting!

✋ Play a fun game of Now You See, Now You Don't. Tape paper plates around the floor. Use one fewer paper plate than there are children. When you say, "Now you can't see," have children close their eyes and mill around the room. Then when you say, "Now you can see," have children uncover their eyes and rush to stand on a paper plate. The child left without a plate to stand on is the next "caller."

Palms in a Bag
We can honor Jesus.

Palms in a Bag
Serves 1

Theme to Remember: Honoring God
Verse to Devour: John 12:13

Simple Supplies:

romaine lettuce leaves

a teaspoon

vinegar

a plastic fork

a resealable plastic sandwich bag

paper towels

sugar

croutons

2 cherry tomatoes (optional)

What to Do:

Rinse the lettuce leaves, and gently pat them with paper towels to dry them. Then tear a large romaine leaf into bite-sized pieces, and place the pieces in the resealable plastic bag. If you desire, rinse 2 cherry tomatoes, and add them to the bag. Sprinkle 1 teaspoon of sugar and 1 teaspoon of vinegar into the bag. Add as many croutons as you like; then seal the bag tightly. Shake your "Palms in a Bag," and then enjoy your salad!

(From Group Publishing, Inc.'s *Incredible Edible Bible Fun;* copyright © 1997 Nanette Goings.)

The Message:

This recipe idea is especially good for Easter.

Set out clean romaine lettuce, paper towels, teaspoons, croutons, sugar, vinegar, plastic forks, cherry tomatoes (optional), and resealable bags. You'll also need an extra lettuce leaf for each child.

Say: **Let's imagine that we're living in the city of Jerusalem during Jesus' time. Jesus is coming today for the Passover Feast, and we're all so excited! Let's run to the city gates to wait for Jesus.** Jog to the other side of the room. Say: **Look! There in the distance, we can see Jesus coming! He's riding on a donkey. Oh, how can we show Jesus that he's important to us? How can we honor him? We can wave palm-tree fronds! They're a symbol of victory.** Give each child a romaine lettuce leaf to wave. **Let's wave our pretend palm leaves and say, "Hosanna! Hosanna! Praise God!"** Lead children in waving their pretend palm leaves. Then say: **Jesus has entered Jerusalem like a king! In fact, Jesus is the king of kings, and we want to honor and praise him.**

Let's make our own "Palms in a Bag" salads; then we'll discover ways to honor God.

Using fresh lettuce leaves, help the kids follow the directions on the recipe card. Toss the lettuce leaves kids waved outside for rabbits to munch. When everyone has made a salad, read aloud John 12:13. Then ask:

● **Why did the people of Jerusalem honor Jesus?**

● **How can we honor Jesus in our lives today?**

Say: **The people of Jerusalem honored Jesus on that first Palm Sunday by waving palm fronds and placing them in the road as Jesus entered the city. We can honor Jesus in our lives today by going to church, worshiping him, and being kind to others. Let's look for new ways to honor Jesus every day.**

Extra Fun:

🖐 You may wish to serve "Palms in a Bag" with "Anointing-Oil Salad Dressing" from page 110.

🖐 Make paper palm fronds by accordion-folding green construction paper into large fan shapes. Tape or staple one end of each fan to make the palm stem. On the crease of each fold, cut lengthwise for four inches. Now wave your "palm fronds" and praise Jesus!

Tears-in-My-Eyes Salsa

Jesus turns our tears to gladness.

Tears-in-My-Eyes Salsa
Serves 10

Theme to Remember:
Joy from Jesus
Verses to Devour: John 20:19-20

Simple Supplies:

1 16-ounce can of diced tomatoes
  with peppers

a mixing bowl

a plastic spoon

tortilla chips

dried, minced onion

a can opener

a tablespoon

paper cups

What to Do:

Open the can of diced tomatoes with peppers, and pour the contents into a mixing bowl. Add 1 tablespoon of the dried, minced onion. Stir to combine the ingredients. Pour the salsa into paper cups, and serve it with tortilla chips. Yum! Yum! (Be sure to refrigerate leftover salsa.)

(From Group Publishing, Inc.'s *Incredible Edible Bible Fun*; copyright © 1997 Nanette Goings.)

The Message:

This is a fun recipe to prepare around Easter.

Set out the cans of diced tomatoes with peppers; dried, minced onion; a can opener; a mixing bowl; tablespoons; plastic spoons; paper cups; and tortilla chips.

Gather the kids together, and ask:

● When were you really sad?
● What made you feel happier?

Say: It's OK to be sad. We might be sad when friends move away, when we lose a favorite toy, or when someone we love dies. When Jesus was put to death on the cross, Jesus' friends were very sad, too. They stood at the foot of the cross and sadly wondered how this could happen. Jesus was the Son of God; he wasn't supposed to die, was he? There must have been tears in their eyes and pain in their hearts. But Jesus' friends didn't know the rest of the story then like we do! Ask:

● What happened three days after Jesus died?

Let children respond, and then say: Jesus rose from death! Jesus was alive, and his friends weren't sad anymore. Jesus took their tears and sadness and turned them to gladness! And Jesus does that for us, too. We know that Jesus can take the greatest pain and sadness inside us and turn it to joy and gladness.

Say: **Let's make "Tears-in-My-Eyes Salsa" to remind us that Jesus turns tears to joy. Then we'll learn more about the joy Jesus brings.**

Help the kids follow the directions on the recipe card to make the salsa. After everyone has had a chance to pour, measure, stir, or serve the salsa, read aloud John 20:19-20. Then ask:

● **How did Jesus turn the disciples' sadness to gladness?**

● **How can Jesus help you when you're sad?**

Say: **Jesus died on the cross to pay the penalty for our sins. What a sad time for us to think about. But Jesus doesn't want us to stay sad. He rose from the dead to show the world that he is the Son of God, the risen Savior. What a happy day that first Easter was!**

Let the kids enjoy the chips and salsa and celebrate that fact that Jesus is alive.

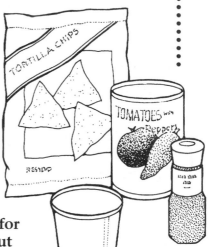

Extra fun:

🖐 Have kids create their own "teardrop" pictures. Let them color pictures with water-based markers. When they're finished, lightly spray the pictures with water. Lay the pictures on newspaper to dry.

🖐 Sing this simple song to the tune of "God Is So Good" the next time you're feeling sad.

When I am sad,

Jesus is near.

When I am sad,

Jesus stays with me.

Heaven's Clouds

Jesus will return to take us to heaven.

Heaven's Clouds
Serves 8

Theme to Remember: Heaven
Verses to Devour: Acts 1:7–11

Simple Supplies:

a 24-ounce tub of cottage cheese

a large bowl

a mixing spoon

paper cups

small container of nondairy whipped topping

a small box of instant vanilla-pudding mix

plastic spoons

What to Do:

Place the cottage cheese into a large bowl. Add the instant vanilla-pudding mix. Stir the pudding mix and cottage cheese until mixed. Gently fold in the nondairy whipped topping. Spoon "Heaven's Clouds" into paper cups, and share this delicious treat with friends.

The Message:

Set out cottage cheese, nondairy whipped topping, instant vanilla-pudding mix, a large bowl, a mixing spoon, plastic spoons, and paper cups.

Ask the children:

● What do you think heaven is like?
● Who lives in heaven?

Say: We know a little about heaven from reading the Bible. Listen as I tell you a Bible story about Jesus' last days on earth.

After Jesus had risen from death, he appeared to his followers and friends. He gave his disciples his last, important instructions. Jesus told the disciples to go into the world and tell others about him. After that, Jesus was carried into heaven to live with God. He disappeared into the clouds as his disciples watched. They were amazed! They worshiped Jesus and then returned to Jerusalem to tell everyone about Jesus.

Say: Jesus is preparing a place for us in heaven even now. Isn't that wonderful? And he's going to return for us someday. Let's make delicious treats called "Heaven's Clouds." Then we'll talk more about Jesus and his return.

Follow the directions on the recipe card. Be sure that each child has a turn to pour, stir, or serve the "clouds." When everyone has been served, read aloud Acts 1:7-11. Then ask:

● **Why did Jesus return to heaven?**

● **What did Jesus want his disciples to do that we can do this week?**

Say: Heaven must be a wonderful place. It's more wonderful than we can even imagine—especially knowing that Jesus is there. And it's great to know that Jesus is coming back someday to take all of us who have faith in him to be with him in heaven!

Extra Fun:

☝ Let kids create watercolor pictures to depict their images of heaven. Talk about the good things we'll experience there.

☝ Make an extra batch of "Heaven's Clouds" to serve to another class. Be sure to tell them the story of Jesus' ascension into heaven. And remember: You're following the instructions Jesus gave his disciples to tell others about him!

Fish-in-the-Sand Spread
Being a Christian can be difficult.

Fish-in-the-Sand Spread
Serves 1

Theme to Remember: Keeping Faith
Verse to Devour: Acts 8:4

Simple Supplies:

measuring spoons

a paper cup

cinnamon

ginger

a plastic knife and a plastic fork

softened margarine

brown sugar

nutmeg

a toothpick

a graham cracker

What to Do:

Measure 1 tablespoon of softened margarine into a paper cup. Add 2 teaspoons of brown sugar, 1/4 teaspoon of cinnamon, 1/8 teaspoon of nutmeg, and 1/8 teaspoon of ginger. Use a fork to smash and mix the ingredients to make edible "sand." Spread a bit of this sand on a graham cracker. With a toothpick, draw a fish shape in the sand. You can also spread your savory sand on a warm piece of toast...yum! yum!

(From Group Publishing, Inc.'s *Incredible Edible Bible Fun*; copyright © 1997 Nanette Goings.)

The Message:

Set out paper cups, softened margarine, brown sugar, cinnamon, nutmeg, ginger, plastic knives and forks, measuring spoons, graham crackers, and toothpicks.

Gather the children together, and ask:

● Have you ever felt that you were in danger?

● Who or what helped you be brave?

Say: In the days after Jesus returned to heaven, being a Christian and loving Jesus was dangerous! Many people didn't love Jesus and wanted to hurt those who did. Some of Jesus' followers were thrown into jail or beaten because they were Christians. But that didn't stop them from telling others about Jesus!

I'm so glad the early Christians didn't stop telling others about Jesus even though it was hard. And even though being a Christian isn't always easy today either, we can have faith that Jesus will help us tell others about him.

In those early days, Christians used the symbol of a fish to secretly identify themselves as Christians. Sometimes they would draw fish symbols in the sand as they stood talking to someone, letting that person know they were Christians. Let's find partners and make special treats called "Fish-in-the-Sand Spread."

Have kids work together with partners, and help them follow the directions on the recipe card. Let each person draw a "fish in the sand" on their graham crackers. When everyone has had a chance to eat his or her cracker with "Fish-in-the-Sand Spread," read aloud Acts 8:4. Then ask:

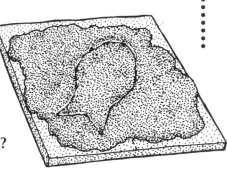

● **In what ways is it hard being a Christian?**
● **What can make being a Christian easier?**
● **What are some ways you can encourage a fellow Christian this week?**

Close with the following prayer. Pray: **Dear God, we know that sometimes it's hard to be Christians. But because of the faith of early Christians, we're able to share our faith with others today. Please help our faith grow and be strong so we can tell people about Jesus and his wonderful love for us. Amen.**

Extra fun:

✍ Have fun making "fish-in-the-sand" pictures. Create a fish shape on a piece of paper using glue. Sprinkle sand over the entire piece of paper, and then shake off the excess sand. When the sandy shape dries, you'll have tactile reminders of the first Christians and of how they told others about Jesus.

✍ Early Christians stuck together and helped each other. Help clean up your Sunday school room or church today. Wipe off tables and chairs, empty wastebaskets, or clean chalkboards.

Open-Eyed Treats
Faith is strongest when we exercise it.

Open-Eyed Treats
Serves 1

Theme to Remember: Faith
Verses to Devour: Acts 9:17-18

Simple Supplies:

2 vanilla wafers

a plastic knife

napkins

a banana

marshmallow creme

gumdrops (optional)

What to Do:

Set out 2 vanilla wafers. Spread marshmallow creme over the vanilla wafers. Place a banana slice on each vanilla wafer as eyes. If you want to add a touch of fun color, use scissors to snip the ends from gumdrops, and place the pieces on the banana slices as pupils.

(From Group Publishing, Inc.'s *Incredible Edible Bible Fun*; copyright © 1997 Nanette Goings.)

The Message:

Set out vanilla wafers, bananas, marshmallow creme, plastic knives, and napkins.

Say: **The Bible has so many exciting stories. One of the most exciting stories is about Paul, who was also called Saul. Let me tell you the story about the time Saul's eyes were opened by Jesus.**

Once there lived a man named Saul.
He didn't like Christians—not at all!
He was always on a Christian patrol.
He'd make them prisoners; that was his goal.
One day a light came down from the sky;
It blinded Saul, and he didn't know why.
Then a voice from above that Saul didn't know
Said, "Saul, why are you hurting me so?"
"Is that you, Lord?" asked Saul, afraid.
"Yes, it is me. Now do what I say."
God sent Saul to Damascus that day.
Blindly Saul went, sure to obey!
While Saul was there, God spoke to a man.
Ananias was his name, and God had a plan.

"Ananias, go to Saul. He's changed, I know."
But Ananias was scared and didn't want to go.
However, his faith was strong in our God,
So he went to Saul with a sigh and a nod.
He laid his hands upon Saul's face,
And then what happened was part of God's grace.
Something fell from over Saul's eyes,
And Saul saw clearly! Oh, what a surprise!
Saul became a Christian that day.
He came to love Jesus and chose to obey.
Saul later was known by the name of Paul,
And he spread God's message to one and all!

Say: That's quite a story, isn't it? When God opens our eyes, we're never the same; we're changed forever! Faith in God helps us see things more clearly.

Let's make "Open-Eyed Treats," and then we'll discover more about faith.

Follow the directions on the recipe card. After everyone has made two pairs of "eyes," read aloud Acts 9:17-18. Then ask:

● Why do you think God blinded Saul? helped Saul see?

● How can trusting God fully in our lives help us serve him better?

Say: Ananias needed faith when God told him to visit Saul. God's power opened the eyes of both of these men in different ways. Both saw God more clearly, and their faith in God grew. We can have stronger faith, too, when we let God open our eyes to his power.

Extra Fun:

Set out chenille wire, tape, and construction paper. Invite kids to make goofy glasses to wear. As kids work, point out that glasses don't help us see God; our faith and our hearts see him!

Good-Fruit Freeze
The Holy Spirit produces good fruit in us.

Good-Fruit Freeze
Serves 1

Theme to Remember:
The fruits of the Spirit
Verses to Devour: Galatians 5:22-23

Simple Supplies:

grape juice

a resealable plastic sandwich bag

a 1/4-cup measuring cup

Vanilla ice cream

an ice-cream scoop

a drinking straw

What to Do:

Place 2 scoops of vanilla ice cream in the resealable plastic bag. Add 1/4 cup of grape juice to the ice cream. Release the excess air from the bag, and then reseal it securely. Press and mix your "Good-fruit freeze" until it's smooth. Open the bag, slide in a straw, and sip.

The Message:

Set out vanilla ice cream, resealable plastic bags, grape juice, drinking straws, measuring cups, and an ice cream scoop.

Gather the kids in a group, and ask:

● What kinds of fruit do you like best?

● What kinds of fruit do you think God likes best?

Say: The Bible tells us that when we have a faith relationship with God through Jesus, God's Spirit lives in us and helps us live the way God wants us to. And when we allow God's Spirit to help us, our lives change, and we concentrate on doing good things. We call the good things that trees produce "fruit." Sometimes we also call the good things the Holy Spirit helps us produce "fruit."

Say: Let's make a fruity treat called "Good-Fruit Freeze." We'll make our treats with grape juice and ice cream, and we'll look at all the "good fruit" things we can do with the Holy Spirit helping us.

Follow the directions on the recipe card. When everyone has made a "Good-Fruit Freeze," read aloud Galatians 5:22-23. Ask:

● What's so good about all these things?

● Why does God want us to produce this fruit in our lives?

● What can you do this week to show God's fruit to people

around you?

Close with the following prayer. Pray: **Dear God, thank you for the relationship we can have with you through Jesus' death on the cross. And thank you that the Holy Spirit lives in us. Help us allow the Holy Spirit to produce good fruit in our lives this week.**

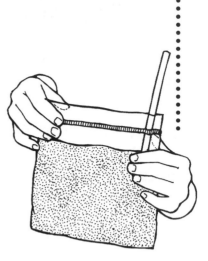

Extra fun:

✋ Share this tasty treat idea with another class to demonstrate to them the good fruit of kindness.

✋ Sing this song to the tune of "Jesus Loves Me" before or after drinking your fruity drinks:

> Jesus loves me, this I know.
>
> For the Bible tells me so.
>
> The Holy Spirit helps me show
>
> These special fruits that I can grow:
>
> Love, joy, and peace,
>
> Patience, kindness, goodness,
>
> Faithfulness, and gentleness,
>
> And even self-control.

Peace-Offering Cocoa

We can be peacemakers.

Peace-Offering Cocoa
Serves 1

Theme to Remember: Peace
Verse to Devour: Philemon 12

Simple Supplies:

a tablespoon

chocolate drink mix

hot tap water

a chocolate candy kiss or heart

powdered milk

a hot-drink cup

a plastic spoon

What to Do:

Measure 2 tablespoons of powdered milk and 1 tablespoon of chocolate drink mix into a hot-drink cup. Add hot tap water to fill the cup 3/4 full, and stir the hot cocoa well. Unwrap the chocolate heart or kiss, drop it into the cup, and then stir until the chocolate has melted. Offer your "Peace-Offering Cocoa" to someone you want to apologize to. Then make yourself another cup!

(From Group Publishing, Inc.'s *Incredible Edible Bible Fun*; copyright © 1997 Nanette Goings.)

The Message:

Set out the powdered milk, chocolate drink mix, hot-drink cups, measuring spoons, plastic spoons, and chocolate hearts or kisses. Set out the hot tap water just before you prepare the cocoa.

Gather the kids together, and ask:

● Have you ever felt unable to say, "I'm sorry"?

● How did you finally apologize?

Say: **The Bible tells us about a time a slave called Onesimus (oh-NES-ih-mus), had stolen from his master, Philemon (fih-LEE-mun). Onesimus ran far away to live and later met the Apostle Paul. The Apostle Paul loved Jesus very much. So when Paul began to teach Onesimus about Jesus, Onesimus realized that when he stole from his master, he had made a big mistake. But he didn't know how to say he was sorry. Paul wanted Onesimus and Philemon to make peace with each other. Paul wrote a letter to Philemon, telling him that Onesimus was now a Christian and that Onesimus realized he had done wrong and now wanted to do what was right. Paul asked Philemon to take Onesimus back and forgive him. The Bible doesn't tell us how the story ended. How do you think it ended?**

Let's make our own "Peace-Offering Cocoa," and then we'll

talk about how we can be peacemakers and forgive others.

Follow the directions on the recipe card. When everyone has made a cup of "Peace-Offering Cocoa," read aloud Philemon 12. Then ask:
- **How did Paul help Onesimus?**
- **Who is a peacemaker that you know?**
- **Who can you forgive or become a peacemaker for this week?**

Close with the following prayer: **Dear God, you have shown us through the story of Paul and Onesimus how we should handle situations where we need forgiveness. Guide us this week. Help us to be peacemakers in all that we do. Amen.**

Extra Fun:

✋ Package up an extra cup of "Peace-Offering cocoa" to give away to a friend. You may want to include a piece of paper with Philemon 12 written on it, too.

✋ Remember these steps when making peace with others:
- —Be kind and loving.
- —Try to see the problem from the other person's point of view.
- —Be committed to solving the problem.
- —Remember, you are both precious children of God.

Anointing-Oil Salad Dressing
We can care for others.

Anointing-Oil Salad Dressing
Serves 12

Theme to Remember:
Caring for others
Verses to Devour: James 5:14-15

Simple Supplies:

vegetable oil

salt

dried herbs such as parsley or paprika

a small, clean jar with a tight-fitting

   lid—a peanut butter jar or a salad

   dressing bottle, for example

cider vinegar

sugar

measuring cups and spoons

What to Do:

Into the jar, pour 1 cup of vegetable oil, 1/3 cup of cider vinegar, 1/2 teaspoon of salt, 1/2 teaspoon of sugar, and 1 tablespoon of dried herbs. Close the jar with a tight-fitting lid, and shake the jar until all the ingredients are well-mixed. Serve the "Anointing-Oil Salad Dressing" on tossed salad or raw vegetables.

(From Group Publishing, Inc.'s *Incredible Edible Bible Fun;* copyright © 1997 Nanette Goings.)

The Message:

Set out vegetable oil, cider vinegar, salt, sugar, herbs, measuring cups and spoons, and a pint jar. You'll also need raw vegetables or tossed salad in bowls for the children. If you wish for each child to take a bit of the salad dressing home, you'll need a clean baby-food jar for each child.

Gather the kids together, and ask:

● Who cares for you when you're sick or hurt?

● How does it make you feel to have someone care for you?

Say: **The Bible tells us about something people did in biblical times to care for those who were sick. They would put a bit of special oil on the person and pray for God to heal the person. They called this "anointing with oil." They did it because they cared about the person and wanted God to heal him or her. Some Christians still anoint people with oil when they pray for healing.**

Let's make "Anointing-Oil Salad Dressing" to remind us that we should care for and pray for people who are hurting.

Help the kids follow the directions on the recipe card. Have everyone help mix the salad dressing in one bottle. While children are taking turns shaking the jar, read aloud James 5:14-15. Then ask:

● How does caring for someone show love?

● What are some ways you can care for others this week?

Close with this prayer. Pray: **Dear God, thank you for sending Jesus to love us and to show us how to care for others. Help us look for ways to be more caring this week. Amen.**

Extra Fun:

☞ Serve "Anointing-Oil Salad Dressing" on "Palms in a Bag" salad. The recipe is found on page 96.

☞ Make an ordinary picture extraordinary with oil. Draw a picture on copier paper with colorful markers. Then squeeze a bit of baby oil onto a cotton ball, and rub the oil over the entire picture. Rub off any excess oil with a paper towel. When the picture is dry, hang it in a window. Your ordinary window will be an extraordinary "stained-glass" window!